# my revision notes

## Edexcel AS and A Level History

# THE USA 1920–55:

## Boom, bust and recovery

Peter Clements

Series editors:
Robin Bunce
Peter Callaghan

HODDER
EDUCATION
AN HACHETTE UK COMPANY

The Publishers would like to thank the following for permission to reproduce copyright material.

**Acknowledgements**

Every effort has been made to trace all copyright holders, but if any have been inadvertently overlooked, the Publishers will be pleased to make the necessary arrangements at the first opportunity.

Although every effort has been made to ensure that website addresses are correct at time of going to press, Hodder Education cannot be held responsible for the content of any website mentioned in this book. It is sometimes possible to find a relocated web page by typing in the address of the home page for a website in the URL window of your browser.

Hachette UK's policy is to use papers that are natural, renewable and recyclable products and made from wood grown in sustainable forests. The logging and manufacturing processes are expected to conform to the environmental regulations of the country of origin.

Orders: please contact Bookpoint Ltd, 130 Milton Park, Abingdon, Oxon OX14 4SE. Telephone: +44 (0)1235 827720. Fax: +44 (0)1235 400454. Email education@bookpoint.co.uk Lines are open from 9 a.m. to 5 p.m., Monday to Saturday, with a 24-hour message answering service. You can also order through our website: www.hoddereducation.co.uk

ISBN: 978 1 4718 7646 2

© Peter Clements 2017

First published in 2017 by

Hodder Education,

An Hachette UK Company

Carmelite House

50 Victoria Embankment

London EC4Y 0DZ

www.hoddereducation.co.uk

Impression number 10  9  8  7  6  5  4  3  2  1

Year        2020  2019  2018  2017  2016

Cover photo © Stocktrek Images, Inc. / Alamy Stock Photo
Illustrations by Integra
Typeset by Integra Software Services Pvt. Ltd., Pondicherry, India
Printed in India

A catalogue record for this title is available from the British Library.

# My revision planner

REVISED

REVISED

# Introduction

## About Paper 2

Paper 2 Option 2H.1 The USA c1920–55: boom, bust and recovery is a depth study. Therefore, it requires a detailed knowledge of the period that you are studying. Paper 2 tests you against two Assessment Objectives: AO1 and AO2.

AO1 tests your ability to:
- organise and communicate your own knowledge
- analyse and evaluate key features of the past
- make supported judgements
- deal with concepts of cause, consequence, change, continuity, similarity, difference and significance

On Paper 2, AO1 tasks require you to write an essay from your own knowledge.

AO2 tests your ability to:
- Analyse and evaluate source material from the past
- To explore the value of source material by considering its historical context

On Paper 2, the AO2 task requires you to write an essay, which analyses two sources from the period you have studied.

At A Level, Paper 2 is worth 20 per cent of your qualification. At AS Level, Paper 2 is worth 40 per cent of your qualification. Significantly, your AS grade does not count towards your overall A Level grade. Therefore, you will have to take this paper at A Level in order to get the A Level qualification.

## Structure

At AS and A Level, Paper 2 is structured around four key topics which cover the period 1920–55. The AS and A Level Exams are divided into two Sections. Section A tests your Source analysis skills, whereas Section B tests your ability to write an essay from own knowledge. Both sections focus on the four key topics. The question may deal with aspects of one of the topics, or may be set on issues that require knowledge of several or all of the topics.

| Aspect of the course | AO | Exam |
|---|---|---|
| Key Topic 1: Boom and crash, 1920–29 | | |
| Key Topic 2: Depression and New Deal, 1935–38 | AO1 & AO2 | Section A and Section B |
| Key Topic 3: Impact of the New Deal and the Second World War on the USA to 1945 | | |
| Key Topic 4: The transformation of the USA 1945–55 | | |

## The exam

At AS and A Level, the Paper 2 exam lasts for 1 hour and 30 minutes. It is divided into two sections, both of which test the depth of your historical knowledge. Section A requires you to answer one compulsory question on two sources. Section B requires you to write one essay. As this is a depth paper, questions can be set on single events or programmes but may cover more extended periods.

## How to use this book

This book has been designed to help you to develop the knowledge and skills necessary to succeed in this exam. The book is divided into four sections – one for each of the Key Topics. Each section is made up of a series of topics organised into double-page spreads. On the left-hand page, you will find a summary of the key content you need to learn. Words in bold in the key content are defined in the glossary. On the right-hand page, you will find exam-focused activities. Together, these two strands of the book will take you through the knowledge and skills essential for exam success.

There are three levels of exam-focused activities:
- Band 1 activities are designed to develop the foundational skills needed to pass the exam.
- Band 2 activities are designed to build on the skills developed in Band 1 activities and to help you achieve a C grade.
- Band 3 activities are designed to enable you to access the highest grades.

Each section ends with an exam-style question and model high-level answer with commentary. This should give you guidance on what is required to achieve the top grades.

# 1 Boom and crash, 1920–29

## The economic boom of the 1920s

The USA emerged from the First World War as the wealthiest country on earth. In the 1920s there was a real sense of prosperity among many sections of the population. Production of industrial goods rose by 50 per cent between 1922 and 1929 and unemployment never rose above 3.7 per cent. However, not all groups shared in the wealth and it was not distributed among all sectors of the economy.

### Changes in industry

Much of industry was becoming modernised in the USA. More industries employed modern manufacturing techniques such as **mass production** and **management science**.

### Mass production

Mass production was based on moving assembly lines. The items being manufactured were brought to workers who completed their part in the production process before they continued on to the next. In this sense, workers contributed to one part of the process rather than manufacturing the goods themselves. This process was most famously developed by motor vehicle manufacturer **Henry Ford** and was facilitated by the development of electricity to power the machines and assembly lines. By 1920 Ford was producing 1,250,000 cars per year or one every 60 seconds. The price of a 'Model T' Ford fell from $950 in 1914, before the introduction of mass production, to $250 by 1925. During the 1920s mass production techniques were used in many industries, such as household goods and textiles. For example, the introduction of standard clothing sizes across the whole of the USA during the First World War made it possible to mass-produce clothing.

### Management science

Different management techniques were developed to run businesses more efficiently. These included developments such as:

● **time and motion techniques** developed by mechanical engineer Frederick W Taylor and his followers in the late nineteenth century. This meant including the timing of productive processes and the setting of productivity targets for employees on this basis.

● The employment of specialist planning and financial departments. One particular development was the growth of business schools. In 1928 there were 89 specialists educating 67,000 students. Most of these students would go on to apply the techniques they had been taught in the schools in the firms which subsequently recruited them.

### Advertising

During the 1920s advertising techniques developed to convince consumers they needed the products on sale. Many companies hired psychologists to design campaigns and target specific groups, for example, 'Lucky Strike' cigarettes were labelled 'torches of freedom' to encourage young women to smoke them in public. By 1929, companies were spending $3 billion annually on advertising.

### Technological advances and their impact on leisure

Technological advances had a huge impact on free time the development of electricity and household appliances meant people had more time for leisure. For example, radio became hugely popular as the first form of entertainment that could be heard at home. Between 1912 and 1929 the number of electrical goods sold per year rose from 1.4 million to 160 million. The development of cinema equally changed people's lives, although the biggest development for many was the automobile.

### The automobile

Mass production made the automobile far more accessible: between 1920 and 1929 the numbers of cars rose from 7.5 million to 27 million. The motor industry was the largest in the USA, dominated by three firms: Ford, General Motors and Chrysler. Cars prompted Americans to see more of their homeland. As a result, greater tourism and hotels developed. Mass production of cars also stimulated road building at the rate of 10,000 miles per year by 1929.

## Spot the mistake

Below are a sample exam question and a paragraph written in answer to this question. Why does this paragraph not get into Level 5? Once you have identified the mistake, rewrite the paragraph so that it displays the qualities of Level 5. The mark scheme on page 102 will help you.

'Technological advances were the crucial factor in generating prosperity in the US in the years 1920–29.' How far do you agree with this statement?

During the 1920s the USA was the wealthiest country in the world. Production of industrial goods rose by 50 per cent between 1922 and 1929 and unemployment remained less than 4 per cent. However not all shared in the wealth equally. More industries employed modern manufacturing techniques such as mass production. This meant more could be produced through the use of moving assembly lines. Henry Ford had developed this technique before the First World War. By 1920 Ford was producing 1,250,000 cars per year. During the 1920s these techniques were used in many industries such as household devices and textiles.

## Complete the paragraph

Below are a sample exam question and a paragraph written in answer to this question. The paragraph contains a point and specific examples, but lacks a concluding analytical link back to the question. Complete the paragraph, adding this link in the space provided.

How far do you agree that the development of new manufacturing techniques was the principal reason for the growing prosperity of the USA in the 1920s?

The development of new manufacturing techniques was the most important reason for the growing prosperity of the USA in the period 1921 to 1929. In particular, these included mass production pioneered by industrialists such as Henry Ford. This meant workers undertook only one part of the productive process, working on items brought to them by a moving production line. The overall result was an increase in production and falling consumer prices. By 1920 Ford's plant could produce a motor car every 60 seconds, while the price fell from $950 in 1914 before the introduction of mass production, to $250 by 1925. During the 1920s many other industries, such as textiles and clothing, applied mass production methods, again with a rise in production and fall in prices. Overall ...

_____

_____

# Government encouragement for business and *laissez-faire* economics

## Republican governments and the economy

The governments in the 1920s were **Republican**. They introduced *laissez-faire* policies that favoured big business. Broadly, they favoured policies such as minimal interference in the economy, low taxes and limited government activity. Governments tended to operate at a **financial surplus** because they spent so little.

The *laissez-faire* approach is particularly associated with President **Calvin Coolidge** (1923–28) and **Andrew Mellon**, Treasury Secretary from March 1921 to February 1932. Both believed wealth filtered down to all classes as the country became more prosperous, so the role of government was to enable business people to operate with minimal regulation.

### *Laissez-faire*

The Government's *laissez-faire* approach meant that they intervened as little as possible in the economy. This resulted in fewer regulations for businesses and low taxes – but the Government didn't accept responsibility in times of **recession** – or for those who did not share in the prosperity.

## Economic policy in the 1920s

The Republican governments pursued policies that actively encouraged business enterprise.

### Tax reductions

The Government reduced taxes in 1924, 1926 and 1928. Mellon gave out tax reductions of $3.5 billion to large-scale industrialists and big corporations during his term of office. These reductions largely favoured the wealthy.

### Fewer regulations

Government interference was minimal, and the numbers of government employees was limited. This meant it was difficult to enforce what regulations there were – such as laws against price fixing between companies to prevent unfair competition. There were few laws protecting labour – children were widely employed, for example, in the textile mills of the South, where 56-hour weeks were common.

### Advantageous foreign markets

Despite the high **tariffs** (see below), the Government encouraged businessmen to invest abroad, particularly in terms of raw materials that fuelled technological developments. Business corporations bought oil concessions in many countries, including Canada and Venezuela, while the large US firm Firestone developed the rubber industry in Liberia, and United Fruit had a larger budget in Costa Rica than its government.

### High tariffs

The Fordney–McCumber tariff, passed in 1922, raised tariffs to cover the difference in costs between imported and domestically produced goods. This made US manufactured goods cheaper in the home market but meant it was difficult to sell them abroad as foreign governments reciprocated with their own high tariffs. The overall effect was to limit foreign trade – and while this was advantageous to US manufacturers in times of domestic boom, they would find it difficult to sell their goods abroad if the home market collapsed.

## Hire purchase

Economic prosperity was in part fuelled by the easy availability of credit. Many goods were bought on hire purchase or easy credit, with a deposit followed by weekly payments. Many of the newly mass produced cars were paid for by hire purchase. By 1929, $7 billion worth of goods were bought on credit. The problem was that people got into debt, and if they failed to meet the payments the goods could be repossessed.

## Select the detail

Below is a sample A Level exam question with the accompanying sources. Having read the question and the Sources, complete the following activity.

How far could the historian make use of Sources 1 and 2 together to investigate the effectiveness of Republican economic policies in the 1920s?

Below are three claims that you could make when answering the question. Read the claims and then select quotes from the sources to support them. Copy down the quotes in the space provided.

Tip: keep the quotes short; never copy more than a sentence. Remember, sometimes a few words embedded in a sentence is all you need to support your claims.

1  The Government's policies were highly effective

_____

_____

2  The Government faced economic problems

_____

_____

3  Source 1 is valuable to a historian as it gives the view of the president of the USA because . . .

_____

_____

### SOURCE 1

From the State of Union Address by President Calvin Coolidge, 1924. Each year US presidents give an account of the state of the country.

Our domestic problems are for the most part economic. We have our enormous debt to pay, and we are paying it. We have the high cost of government to diminish, and we are diminishing it. We have a heavy burden of taxation to reduce, and we are reducing it. But while remarkable progress has been made in these directions, the work is yet far from accomplished. We still owe over $21,000,000,000, the cost of the National Government is still about $3,500,000,000, and the national taxes still amount to about $27 for each one of our inhabitants. There yet exists this enormous field for the application of economy.

### SOURCE 2

From an address during the presidential election campaign by Republican candidate Herbert Hoover in Newark, New Jersey, 17 September 1928.

When we [the Republican Party] assumed direction of the Government in 1921 there were five to six million unemployed men upon our streets. Wages and salaries were falling and hours of labor increasing... The Republican Administration at once undertook to find relief to this situation. At once a nationwide employment conference was called... Within a year we restored these five million workers to employment. But we did more; we produced a fundamental program which made this restored employment secure on foundation of prosperity; as a result wages and standards of living have during the past six and a half years risen to steadily higher levels.

This recovery and this stability are no accident. It has not been achieved by luck. Were it not for sound governmental policies and wise leadership, employment condition in America today would be similar to those existing in many other parts of the world.

# Limits to the boom

Not all groups shared in the prosperity of the 1920s. In particular, farmers and black Americans missed out.

## Farmers

Agriculture had performed well during the First World War when demand was high and prices had risen by over 25 per cent. However, the end of the war led to falling demand, therefore wheat prices fell from $2.5 to $1 per bushel.

### Reasons for declining demand

- **Prohibition** reduced demand for grain used in the manufacture of alcohol.
- The growth of **synthetic fibres** reduced the demand for textile crops such as cotton.
- The introduction of more machinery and modern methods meant more could be produced on less **acreage**. Indeed, during the 1920s, 13 million acres were taken out of production, yet overall production increased by nine per cent.
- High foreign tariffs reduced demand for US agricultural produce abroad.
- Conditions for small farmers were made worse by the growth of agri-businesses: large-scale, machinery intensive farms, which required little labour except at harvest times.

The result of declining demand was overproduction, which kept prices low. Possibly as many as 66 per cent of farms operated at a loss. Often farmers were in debt to the banks who ceased to lend to them when they couldn't meet mortgage repayments. Government policy was to lend money through the Agricultural Credits Act 1923, placing small farmers in even more debt.

## Agricultural Credits Act 1923

Farmers were encouraged to co-operate to market their produce together. The Act gave loans to farming co-operatives. Large agricultural businesses were best able to take advantage of loans to produce more efficiently, thus squeezing small farmers even harder.

## Black Americans

Around 85 per cent of black Americans still lived in the South, the poorest part of the USA. Many were sharecroppers, eking out a precarious living and paying a percentage of their produce as rent. Black Americans constituted 14 per cent of small farmers, while accounting in 1930 for less than 10 per cent of the total population.

Others moved north to find work in the industrial cities such as Chicago. However, even here black Americans faced discrimination in employment and housing. Most were limited to the lowest paid, most menial jobs such as street cleaning. Often they were concentrated in '**ghettoes**' such as Harlem in New York whose black American population grew from 50,000 in 1914 to 165,000 by 1930.

In much of the South and Midwest black Americans were terrorised by racist groups such as the Ku Klux Klan (see page 16).

## Unequal distribution of the boom

The prosperity of the 1920s was very much associated with the industrial North and far West of the USA. In 1929 the **per capita incomes** of these two regions was $921 and $881 respectively: the figure in the south-east was $365. Indeed, income distribution might be becoming more unequal: one 1929 survey found 60 per cent of families had incomes of less than $2,000. Furthermore, even in the more prosperous regions, employment could be unstable: sociologists Robert and Helen Lynd found 72 per cent of families surveyed in 1924 in Muncie, Indiana had been unemployed at some stage.

**Delete as applicable**

Below are a sample exam question and a paragraph written in answer to this question. Read the paragraph and decide which of the possible options (in bold) is most appropriate. Delete the least appropriate options and complete the paragraph by justifying your selection.

'The economic boom of the 1920s led to widespread prosperity in the US.' How far do you agree with this statement?

The prosperity in the USA was **very/partially/not at all** widespread. Many groups missed out on the prosperity, notably non-whites such as native and black Americans. The agricultural sector generally remained depressed as a result of overproduction and falling prices. Even within the industrial areas there was uncertainty. In 1924 sociologists Robert and Helen Lynd found that 72 per cent of families had experienced unemployment at some point. Meanwhile, there were marked differences in per capita income by different regions, with that of the industrial North almost three times higher than that of the mainly rural Southeast. The prosperity was therefore **widely spread/unevenly spread/concentrated in certain areas** because …

_____

_____

 **Support or challenge?**

Below is a sample exam question which asks how far you agree with a specific statement. Below this are a series of general statements, which are relevant to the question. Using your own knowledge and the information on the opposite page decide whether these statements support or challenge the statement in the question and circle the appropriate response.

How far do you agree that the population of the USA enjoyed widespread and sustained prosperity during the 1920s?

| | Support | Challenge |
|---|---|---|
| There was increased use of many technological developments such as mass production | | |
| More efficient methods of management and marketing were developed | | |
| Unemployment remained low | | |
| Agriculture as a whole did not share in the prosperity although profitable agri-businesses grew | | |
| Members of ethnic groups remained relatively poor | | |
| There were widespread differences between the overall prosperity of different regions. | | |

# Causes of the Wall Street Crash of 1929

## Problems in the economy

In October 1929 the **Wall Street Stock Exchange** crashed. On 29 October, 16,410,030 shares were sold as their price collapsed: by mid November $30 billion had been lost. The Wall Street Crash had a series of causes.

## Overproduction

The economic boom was dependent on continuous production, which was in turn dependent on continuous demand. However, by the late 1920s demand was falling as more goods were produced than could be sold. People simply couldn't afford to buy more. As a result, more workers were laid off or worked part time. One survey in 1929 estimated that the incomes of 80 per cent of Americans were so low that they lived close to **subsistence** even when they were in work.

## The construction industry

The health of the construction industry is often given as an indicator of the health of the economy as a whole. By the late 1920s, the construction industry was in recession. Indeed, by the end of the decade construction workers were often employed on part-time contracts, and there was a reduced demand for building materials.

## Land speculation

There had been considerable **speculation** in land, particularly in Florida. As increased mobility through the development of road transport made Florida more accessible, land values soared and people invested in new resorts and developments. However, demand tailed off and values began to fall: this coincided with a devastating hurricane in 1926, which destroyed many of the developments and left many investors severely out of pocket. By 1926 the Florida Land Boom was over.

## The bull market

During the late 1920s, demand for shares grew considerably. This created a condition known as the **bull market**. Demand for shares was based on the assumption that share prices would continue to rise. Many bought shares on credit – a 10 per cent deposit and the remainder on weekly payments – known as 'buying on the margin'. However, if the boom collapsed they would be left with valueless shares that they still had to continue paying for at the price of their original investment.

The Stock Market was also relatively unregulated, so unscrupulous brokers could speculate and involve themselves in **insider dealing** to make prices rise and fall artificially. While this enabled some members to make huge profits, it again left more gullible investors with worthless stock.

## Weaknesses of the banking system

The US banking system was outdated and largely unregulated.

- In 1913 the **Federal Reserve** System, also known as 'the Fed', had been created, with 12 Federal Reserve Banks given responsibility to monitor and regulate the entire banking system. However, they inevitably operated in their own interests rather than those of the nation as a whole.
- National banks were regulated by the Federal Reserve System. However, there were also 30,000 relatively small local banks, which remained completely outside the Reserve bank system. In some cases, they issued their own currencies, which would only be accepted in their local areas, and were completely unprotected against collapse. A **run on the bank** could see their investors lose all their savings.

In order to keep the economy buoyant, the Federal Reserve System favoured low interest rates. But this fuelled easy credit and the increasing amounts of debt to which many were subject.

## ! Mind map

Use the information on the opposite page to add detail to the mind map below to help you understand what caused the Wall Street Crash.

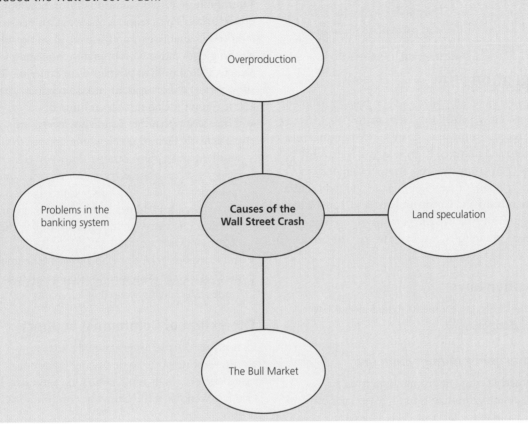

## ♦ Eliminate irrelevance    **a**

Below are a sample exam question and a paragraph written in answer to this question. Read the paragraph and identify parts of the paragraph that are not directly relevant to the question. Draw a line through the information that is irrelevant and justify your deletions in the margin.

> How far were the problems of the Bull Market responsible for the Wall Street Crash of October 1929?

The problems of the Bull Market were to a large degree responsible for the Wall Street Crash of October 1929. The 1920s saw a huge growth in the buying and selling of shares, a situation known as the Bull Market. Many people bought shares, expecting their value to rise. Often they bought shares on the margin, or on credit. Some lost track of how many shares they had or how much they were paying for them. They didn't understand the system and didn't understand they could still be left paying for valueless shares if their price on the Stock Market did fall. The Stock Market was unregulated, enabling unscrupulous brokers to speculate and practise insider dealing, thus enabling stocks prices to rise or fall artificially. They might do this by selling them to each other to raise prices and then agreeing to sell them all at once. Many would then be left with shares of little value. Clearly, the Stock Exchange was not built on solid foundations and if the economic boom collapsed, the value of shares would plummet. However, the Wall Street Crash was not caused by problems within the Stock Market itself. Other factors needed to be considered.

# Changes in society: immigration and the Red Scare

The 1920s saw significant changes taking place in society. More conservative people, especially in rural areas, often felt threatened by these. They also feared what they perceived as alien influences, particularly from more recent immigrants.

## Immigration

Traditionally, the USA prided itself on being a nation of immigrants. However, by the 1920s many people feared the more recent immigrants. They viewed immigrants from eastern and southern Europe as 'un-American', because of their ethnicity, their Roman Catholic or Orthodox religion, or their commitment to radical ideas such as **anarchism** and **Communism**. Also, hard-working immigrants from Asia had the potential to become highly successful in the USA, and threaten the privileged position of white people.

## Immigration laws

During the 1920s, governments passed several laws restricting immigration.

### 1921 Emergency immigration law

This imposed a ceiling of immigration from any European country, limiting it to three per cent of nationals living in the USA in 1911. This clearly favoured western European countries such as Britain who had large numbers in the USA, while **New Immigrants** from southern and eastern Europe were still arriving.

### 1924 Johnson–Reed Act

The 1924 Johnson–Reed Act banned immigration from Japan. Immigration into the USA from other Asian groups had already been banned in the late nineteenth century.

## Red Scare

The **Red Scare** is particularly associated with the fears outlined by **A Mitchell Palmer**, Attorney General from 1919 to 1921, concerning the threat of a Communist revolution in the USA.

## Background

After the First World War, inflation and the upheaval of a return to a peacetime economy caused considerable industrial unrest both among members of the white working class and new immigrants. For example, at one time in 1919 4 million workers were on strike. There was also a series of assassinations and assassination attempts on public figures including Palmer himself.

- Threats of violent revolution however were particularly blamed on 'new immigrants' from southern and eastern Europe. Attorney General Palmer clearly saw the latter as trying to create a Communist revolution in the USA. This became the 'Red Scare'. In the so-called 'Palmer Raids', 6,000 were arrested. The vast majority were quickly released in the absence of any evidence against them.
- In December 1919, the USS *Buford*, nicknamed the 'Soviet Ark', was used to deport to Russia 249 'undesirable' aliens accused of left-wing views.

## The extent of Communist support

Commentators also exaggerated the extent of Communist support – some placing Communist membership as high as 600,000. One authority, Professor Gordon Watkins of the University of Illinois was more realistic at 100,000 – or one-fifth of one per cent of the population. Many at the time confused industrial action, which was simply about better pay and working conditions, with the political radicalism of Communists.

Cynics believed Palmer was promoting the idea of the scare to support his own attempt to run for the presidency. However, many across the USA believed the credibility of his concerns and had a genuine fear of imminent revolution. Nonetheless, when Palmer warned of a huge Communist demonstration to take place on 20 May 1920, which never in fact materialised, the Red Scare died away. Fears lingered, however, and many people remained circumspect in terms of their beliefs in case they were accused of supporting radicalism.

## Saccho and Vanzetti

Saccho and Vanzetti were two Italian-Americans who were accused in 1920 of an armed robbery. Both professed to be anarchists, and although there was little evidence against them, and despite a massive campaign to have them acquitted, they were executed in 1927.

**Simple essay style**

Below is a sample exam question. Use your own knowledge and the information on the opposite page to produce a plan for this question. Choose four general points, and provide three pieces of specific information to support each general point. Once you have planned your essay, write the introduction and conclusion for the essay. The introduction should list the points to be discussed in the essay. The conclusion should summarise the key points and justify which point was the most important.

'The Red Scare was both a cause and effect of widespread fears of immigration in the 1920s'. How far do you agree with this statement?

 **RAG – rate the factors**                    **a**

Below are a sample exam question and a series of factors, which could be used in answer to it. Read the question, study the factors and, using three coloured pens, put a Red, Amber or Green star next to the events to show:

- Red: events and policies that have no relevance to the question
- Amber: events and policies that have some significance to the question
- Green: events and policies that are directly relevant to the question

1 How accurate is it to say that US society underwent significant tensions during the 1920s?
- Warren Harding was elected as the first of three successive Republican presidents in 1920.
- Many rural people distrusted social developments in urban areas.
- Many people feared immigration and measures were taken to limit it.
- Many more recent immigrants from Southern and Eastern Europe were suspected of Communist sympathies.
- There was a widespread 'Red Scare' in the early 1920s.
- Attorney General Mitchell Palmer wanted to run for president.
- Saccho and Vanzetti were accused of robbery and murder.

Now repeat the activity with the following questions:

2 How far was the Red Scare a reaction to fears about changes in US society?

3 'The US underwent profound social change during the 1920s.' How far do you agree with this statement?

# The Ku Klux Klan

The Ku Klux Klan was a racist organisation formed in the aftermath of the civil war that aimed to maintain white supremacy over former slaves. Membership proliferated in small-town and rural USA during the 1920s, gaining 100,000 followers by 1921.

## Beliefs and methods

The Ku Klux Klan advocated white supremacy and attacked blacks, Jews, Catholics and anyone it felt was supporting un-American ideas. It opposed what it considered to be foreign or immoral influences such as jazz music.

The Klan held rallies and marches to demonstrate their presence and practised acts of brutality against all those who opposed their views. In particular, they terrorised black Americans in the hope they would remain at the lowest strata of society. The Klan committed acts of violence and even murder.

## Leadership

Two of the leaders of the Klan, Edgar Clark and Elizabeth Tyler were professional fundraisers and publicity agents who put their skills to good use. Effectively, they exploited their membership, charging recruits $10 to join, $6.50 for robes manufactured by a Klan-controlled company for $3.28, and selling printed material published exclusively by the Klan-run Searchlight Publishing Company at a vast profit.

## Membership

Most Klan supporters were less affluent people who feared change and foreign influences. The secretive rituals, violence, group membership and activities gave a sense of excitement to their lives. This was recognised by Hiram Wesley Evans, a Texas dentist who succeeded as leader in 1924. Evans reported that supporters were the descendants of the pioneers and should have been at the apex of US society, but saw foreigners and black Americans threatening to overtake them in status.

## Influence

During the peak of popularity, the Klan could control both politicians and police in certain areas. It is alleged that in 1924 it helped elect governors in Maine, Ohio, Colorado and Louisiana. Nevertheless, the Klan had little influence in bigger cities where many people may have been more sophisticated in their views.

The Klan did however maintain a national profile, often through large-scale parades in big cities: over 50,000 for example marched through Washington DC on 13 September 1926.

## Impact on black Americans

While the Klan succeeded in terrorising many black Americans, it also stimulated the migration of black Americans north to industrial cities (see page 10). The Klan's actions encouraged many to sympathise with its victims and where possible join separatist organisations such as Marcus Garvey's Universal Negro Improvement Society (see page 22).

## Collapse of the Ku Klux Klan

The Klan collapsed because of corruption within its own ranks.
- Leaders made a fortune from the marketing of robes, periodicals and the other paraphernalia of membership.
- The Klan was rocked by scandal. One of its most charismatic leaders, David Stevenson of Indiana was accused of second degree murder following the suicide of a lady he was alleged to have raped.
- There was considerable financial mismanagement with leaders enjoying lavish lifestyles, investing in land and buying luxury yachts. There were revelations of financial corruption by Klan leaders in the state of Pennsylvania.

By 1929, Klan membership had fallen to 20,000. Its leadership attempted to turn it into a social club by emphasising outdoor activities such as camping as opposed to its political role and propensity to violence. Many felt it had gone soft; others felt it was increasingly irrelevant.

However, for many, the racist ideas which had informed the membership remained and those with differing views of membership of ethnic minorities still faced violence and intimidation in the South and more rural areas.

**Explain the difference**                                                     **a**

The following sources give different attitudes towards the Ku Klux Klan. List the ways in which the sources differ. Explain the differences between the sources using the provenance of the sources and the historical context. The provenance appears at the top of the source. Make sure you stay focused on the differences that are relevant to the question.

How far could the historian make use of Sources 1 and 2 together to investigate attitudes towards the Ku Klux Klan during the years 1921–29?

Explain your answer, using both sources, the information given about them and your own knowledge of the historical context.

## SOURCE 1

From 'The Klan: Defender of Americanism', Hiram Wesley Evans, the leader or Imperial Wizard of the Ku Klux Klan, published in the magazine *The Forum*, December 1925.

We of the Klan believe that we can prove our case to all who will agree with us on one fundamental thing. It is this: We believe that the pioneers who built America bequeathed to their own children a priority right to it, the control of it and of its future, and that no one on earth can claim any part of this inheritance except through our generosity. We believe, too, that the mission of America under Almighty God is to perpetuate and develop just the kind of nation and just the kind of civilization which our forefathers created. This is said without offense to other civilizations, but we do believe that ours, through all possible growth and expansion, should remain the same kind that was 'brought forth upon this continent'. Also, we believe that races of men are as distinct as breeds of animals; that any mixture between races of any great divergence is evil; that the American stock, which was bred under highly selective surroundings, has proved its value and should not be mongrelized...

## SOURCE 2

From 'Is the Ku Klux Un-American?', William Robinson Pattangall, a Democratic politician from the state of Maine, published in the magazine *The Forum*, September 1925.

Americanism, of course, is really an ideal and a spirit – a faith in freedom, tolerance, humanity. It cannot discriminate because of color, birthplace, or creed; nor can it tolerate caste, class, or religious distinctions in politics, social life, or legal standing; especially it cannot for a moment endure the breeding and exploitation of hatred and prejudice as a means to sway public opinion and win political power. The Klan, on its own statement, does just these things, and makes a virtue of doing them... Equally un-American is its practice of attempting secret and threatening influence on the Government. No one has shown how great this evil is more clearly than the Klan speakers themselves; then they turn about and try to do the same thing, not merely as a reprisal, but as a permanent method in American politics. The Klan seeks a secret hold on legislators, judges, and other officials. It uses that hold to enforce its own demands, abandoning completely the American principle of rule by and for all. It maintains expensive lobbies, it acts secretly in both parties, it tries constantly for control secret control of elections, legislatures, and government. And again it has the effrontery to advertise all this as a great principle.

## Recommended reading

- Robert Coughlin, 'Konklave in Kokomo', in (ed) Isabel Leighton, *The Aspirin Age*, pages 115–140 (1964 edition)
- Lucy Moore, *Anything Goes*, pages 188–214 (2008)
- Michael E Parrish, *Anxious Decades*, Part One: Chapter 6 (1992)

# The changing role of women

On the surface the period of the 1920s offered new opportunities to women, particularly in the workplace and in social life. However, while employment opportunities rose, few women enjoyed managerial positions, and long-term aspirations widely focused on marriage and childcare.

## Politics

Women enjoyed limited political opportunities. Although the 19th Amendment of 1920 gave them the right to vote, their political voice was muted.

While women held 145 seats on the various **state legislatures** in 1928, only two out of 435 delegates in the **House of Representatives** were female, with no female senators.

## Employment

Some women found success in the film industry and fashion, although the numbers were small. Women found plentiful employment in such professions as office-work as clerks and typists. However, it was rare for them to move up to managerial positions, and for those who did, it was often at the sacrifice of marriage and family.

### Professions

By 1930 there were only 150 women dentists and fewer than 100 female accountants in the USA.

The vast majority of working women were in low-paid employment such as shop work or clerical, or in menial jobs such as domestic service. Many of these women were black Americans. Even when women did the same jobs as men they received less pay.

## Women's issues

Women were increasingly concerned with issues such as birth control and healthcare, championed by the American Birth Control League, but largely found government and conservative voices unsympathetic. One of the few measures aimed at women was the 1921 Sheppard–Towner Act, which gave states federal aid to develop healthcare for pregnant women. However, many feminists believed this simply reinforced the role of women as child bearers and detracted from the need for birth control.

## Flappers

There was considerable media interest in so-called liberated young women, nicknamed '**Flappers**' who enjoyed a hedonistic lifestyle in the 1920s. Many were shocked by the idea of women attending public places unchaperoned, dancing, smoking and flaunting Prohibition. However, Flappers were confined to large towns and cities and it was a transient phase. Liberated social behaviour did not provide more career opportunities or equal treatment – and as the 1920s progressed most settled to domesticity.

## Traditional views

Many women remained traditional in their views. In the later Muncie survey of 1929, 89 per cent of girls said they would like a job but would relinquish it in marriage, while educational institutions focused very much on domestic skills. One of the few women administrators at the all-female Vassar College herself argued that the college should provide education concomitant with the principal female concerns of childcare and the home.

## Explain the difference

The following sources give different accounts of the role and status of women in the 1920s. List the ways in which the sources differ. Explain the differences between the sources using the provenance of the sources, and the historical context. The provenance appears at the top of the source. Make sure you stay focused on the differences that are relevant to the A Level question below.

How far could the historian make use of Sources 1 and 2 together to investigate the changing role and status of women in the 1920s?

Explain your answer, using both sources, the information given about them and your own knowledge of the historical context.

### SOURCE 1

From *Hail Columbia!: Random Impressions of a Conservative English Radical,* by Walter Lionel George, 1921. (W. L. George was an English writer who travelled extensively through the USA in the 1920s.)

I have been equally surprised by the conquests made in business by American women. It is rather a shock to a European to meet a pretty girl of twenty-seven, to hear that she is employed in a drug corporation, and then to discover that she is a director. A shock to find a woman running a lawyer's office entailing annual expenses of seven or eight thousand dollars, and making a living. It is a surprise to find the American stenographer earning four times as much as her European sister. All those shocks, however, arise out of particular instances, and, though I agree that the American woman has made herself a good position, when I go through a business reference book I find that not one in a hundred of the leading names is the name of a woman. In America man still rules; all you can say is that he does not rule women so harshly as he does in Europe.

### SOURCE 2

From 'Evils of Woman's Revolt against the Old Standards', an article written by Rev. Hugh L. McMenamin, a Roman Catholic priest of conservative views, in the periodical *Current History* in October 1927.

Look about you. The theatre, the magazine, the current fiction, the ballroom, the night clubs and the joyrides—all give evidence of an ever-increasing disregard for even the rudiments of decency in dress, deportment, conventions [standards], and conduct. Little by little the bars have been lowered, leaving out the few influences that held society in restraint. One need be neither prude nor puritan to feel that something is passing in the hearts and in the minds of the women of today that is leaving them cold and unwomanly...

We may try to deceive ourselves and close our eyes to the prevailing flapper conduct. We may call boldness greater self-reliance, brazenness greater self-assertion, license greater freedom, and try to pardon immodesty in dress by calling it style and fashion, but the fact remains that deep down in our hearts we feel a sense of shame and pity... Modern economic conditions, with the mania for speedy profits, have been a powerful factor in producing the 'New Woman'. inasmuch as they have dragged her into the commercial world and made her economically independent. It is quite impossible for a woman to engage successfully in business and politics and at the same time create a happy home. A woman cannot be a mother and a typist at the same time, and unfortunately she elects to be merely a wife, and out of that condition have arisen those temples of race suicide—our modern apartment houses—and the consequent grinding of the divorce mills.

# Prohibition and organised crime

In 1918 the 18th Amendment banned the sale, transportation and manufacture of intoxicating liquor within the USA in order to end consumption of alcohol. This was Prohibition. It was widely supported in rural and small-town USA, by conservative and religious groups, but was generally a failure and led to the rise of organised crime.

## Reasons for Prohibition

Prohibition was supported by a wide variety of interest groups.

- Many women's groups argued that alcohol consumption was a means by which men oppressed them.
- Big business owners claimed that drunkenness was a cause of dangers and inefficiency in the workplace.
- Many religious groups believed that alcohol was a cause of immoral behaviour.

Despite widespread support, Prohibition was widely flaunted and many considered it a failure.

## Why Prohibition failed

Prohibition failed to achieve the results that its supporters had expected as:

- it was impossible to police the 18,700 miles of US coastline and was therefore easy to smuggle in alcohol from abroad
- bootleggers manufactured and distributed alcohol illegally
- alcohol for industrial purposes was legal so it was easy to divert this into alcoholic drinks
- Treasury Agents charged with the enforcement of Prohibition were poorly resourced and paid.

It was estimated than less than five per cent of illegal alcohol was intercepted, while the profits from the illicit industry were $2 billion per year.

## Crime and gangsterism

Prohibition led to a huge rise in the growth of organised crime and gangsterism. Mobsters controlled territory by force and established monopolies of manufacture and distribution in these areas. Disputes led to gang wars. Chicago in particular became notorious for crime.

### Al Capone

One of the leading gangsters in Chicago was **Al Capone**. He insisted he did not force anyone to drink alcohol and he was only meeting demand. He dealt with competitors ruthlessly, however, as exemplified by the St Valentine's Day Massacre in 1929 when members of a rival gang were killed. His 700-strong gang was responsible for over 300 murders in the Chicago region alone. When Capone was finally jailed in 1932 it was estimated that his gang had done $70 million worth of business.

## Prohibition: success and failure

### Success of Prohibition

Prohibition was more successful in rural and small-town areas where it received wide support. Many areas remained 'dry'. It has been credited, albeit without satisfactory evidence for factors such as

- the fall in numbers of road deaths as a result of drunken driving
- the fall in numbers of convictions for drunken behaviour
- improvements in safety in the workplace.

### Failure of Prohibition

Prohibition criminalised millions of people who simply wanted a drink. Some saw it as an attack on working-class consumption of alcohol. It was mainly working-class saloons that were shut down: the prices in the speakeasies where alcohol was consumed ensured the clientele was mainly middle class.

Even when Prohibition was abolished, organised crime continued. Gangs continued to involve themselves in gambling, prostitution and drugs.

### End of Prohibition

The Wickersham Committee, appointed in May 1929 to investigate the effectiveness of Prohibition, acknowledged it couldn't be enforced despite taking up 66 per cent of the entire law enforcement budget. **President Roosevelt** abolished it in 1933. The 20th Amendment made it the responsibility of individual states to decide the issue and most were quick to allow alcohol for consumption.

## ! Simple essay style

Below is a sample exam question. Use your own knowledge and the information on the opposite page to produce a plan for this question. Choose four general points, and provide three pieces of specific information to support each general point. Once you have planned your essay, write the introduction and conclusion for the essay. The introduction should list the points to be discussed in the essay. The conclusion should summarise the key points and justify which point was the most important.

How accurate is it to say that Prohibition was primarily responsible for the massive rise in organised crime that took place in the USA in the 1920s?

## ⸙ Identify an argument    a

Below are a series of definitions, a sample exam question and two sample conclusions. One of the conclusions achieves a high mark because it contains an argument. The other achieves a lower mark because it contains only description and assertion. Identify which is which. The mark scheme on page 102 will help you.

- Description: a detailed account.
- Assertion: a statement of fact or an opinion which is not supported by a reason.
- Reason: a statement which explains or justifies something.
- Argument: an assertion justified with a reason.

How accurate is it to say that Prohibition failed to achieve the aims of its creators in the period 1920 to 1929?

Prohibition failed to achieve the aims of its creators to end the consumption of alcohol among all classes. Indeed, it may have led to a rise in consumption. However, its effects were uneven among differing groups of people and different areas of the USA. Some saw it more as an attack on working-class consumption of alcohol than a ban on alcohol in total. It was mainly working-class saloons that were shut down: the prices in the speakeasies where alcohol was consumed ensured the clientele was mainly middle class. However, the measure was successful in some respects. Many rural areas where support for it was high — for example, in the 'Bible belt' of the South and Midwest — remained 'dry'. It also had a positive impact, for example, leading to fewer deaths from drunken driving or workplace accidents as a result of drink.

Prohibition was the banning of the sale of alcohol as a result of the 18th Amendment of 1918. It failed for various reasons. It was easy for smugglers to bring in alcohol illegally. Alcohol for industrial purposes was legal, so it was easy to divert this into alcoholic drinks. Treasury Agents charged with the enforcement of Prohibition were poorly resourced and paid.

# Cultural change in the 1920s

During the 1920s there were significant changes in US culture, from a wider interest in and respect for aspects of black American culture to a sense of disillusionment which fuelled some of the greatest US literature.

## The Jazz age

Jazz was the defining sound of US cities in the 1920s. It was rooted in black American musical traditions. In the 1920s jazz became more mainstream, as musicians such as Louis Armstrong provided the rhythms for new dance crazes such as the Charleston and Black Bottom. In America's cities, nightclubs attracted young people, especially 'Flappers', while jazz music could be heard in the home for the first time through radio and records. Many older people felt jazz encouraged immorality in the young, particularly as it had its origins in black American culture.

## The Harlem Renaissance

During the 1920s Harlem was a predominantly black neighbourhood in New York. The area had problems such as overcrowding, poor living conditions and crime. At the same time, it also gave rise to an explosion of new culture, which became known as the Harlem Renaissance.

Harlem was home to night clubs such as the Cotton Club featuring top class jazz and blues artistes such as Armstrong and Duke Ellington, which attracted a largely white clientele. It was also a centre of black intellectuals such as:

- Jessie Redmon Fauset, a writer, editor and campaigner for black empowerment
- Alain Locke and Langston Hughes who challenged racial stereotypes through poetry
- Zora Neale Hurston, a novelist and anthropologist.

## The New Negro

The New Negro movement was very much associated with the Harlem Renaissance; some intellectuals associated with the movement advocated **separatism**. Marcus Garvey's Universal Negro Improvement Society, for example, advocated not only separatism within the USA but also migration to Africa. This was opposed by organisations such as the **National Association for the Advancement of Colored People (NAACP)**.

## 'The making of Harlem'

James Weldon Johnson, a black American poet first promoted the Harlem Renaissance in a 1925 essay, 'The Making of Harlem'. The essay publicised economic success stories, such as 'Pigfoot Mary' who made a fortune selling fast food on street corners, but also the resurgence of African American culture. Through this the work of influential black poets such as Alain Locke and Langston Hughes became much more widely known to white audiences with the hope that an appreciation of black American literature, arts and music would lead white people to question their racists assumptions.

Other black Americans meanwhile decried white interest in Harlem, regarding themselves as animals in a zoo, and speaking of '**white tourism**'.

## American literature

US literature enjoyed widespread admiration in the 1920s with writers such as Ernest Hemingway and F Scott Fitzgerald at the height of their influence. They were disillusioned with US society, believing it too materialistic and focused on economic growth. They showed in novels such as *The Great Gatsby* (by Scott Fitzgerald, 1925) and *The Sun Also Rises* (by Hemingway, 1926) however, that the alternative was no better. Both Hemingway and Scott Fitzgerald showed the emptiness of lives without moral purpose, of people who were living outside mainstream society and money-making but still disillusioned. Sinclair Lewis, meanwhile, showed in novels such as *Main Street* and *Babbitt* that any attempts to escape were doomed to failure.

However, most people read popular escapist fiction such as Zane Grey westerns and periodicals such as *Reader's Digest*. They simply wanted undemanding entertainment.

## Explain the difference

**a**

The following sources give different accounts of black American attitudes to segregation. List the ways in which the sources differ. Explain the differences between the sources using the provenance of the sources, and the historical context. The provenance appears at the top of the source. Make sure you stay focused on the differences that are relevant to the A Level question below.

> How far could the historian make use of Sources 1 and 2 together to investigate the attitudes of black America to racial integration during the 1920s?

> Explain your answer, using both sources, the information given about them and your own knowledge of the historical context.

### SOURCE 1

From a speech by Marcus Garvey, 'If you think the negro has a soul', delivered in 1921. Garvey was speaking to a largely black American audience who may have been sympathetic to his views favouring the separation of ethnic groups.

It is for me to inform you that the Universal Negro Improvement Association is an organization that seeks to unite, into one solid body, the four hundred million Negroes in the world. To link up the fifty million Negroes in the United States of America, with the twenty million Negroes of the West Indies, the forty million Negroes of South and Central America, with the two hundred and eighty million Negroes of Africa, for the purpose of bettering our industrial, commercial, educational, social, and political conditions... We of the Universal Negro Improvement Association are raising the cry of "Africa for the Africans," those at home and those abroad... The great problem of the Negro for the last 500 years has been that of disunity. No one or no organization ever succeeded in uniting the Negro race. But within the last four years, the Universal Negro Improvement Association has worked wonders. It is bringing together in one fold four million organized Negroes who are scattered in all parts of the world.

### SOURCE 2

From Robert W. Bagnall, 'The Madness of Marcus Garvey', *Messenger*, March 1923. Bagnall was a senior official in the National Association for the Advancement of Coloured People (NAACP, see page 89) and a church minister in Detroit. In 1922 he joined the 'Garvey Must Go' movement.

He [Garvey] states that his organization has 4,500,000 members and is all over the world. An analysis of his financial report of 1921 reveals that he has not 20,000 dues paying members, and that his paying membership is much smaller than the National Association for the Advancement of Colored People.

He stated that 150,000 delegates would attend his convention. No more than 200 delegates were present as revealed by a careful analysis of the vote, day by day as given in the *Negro World*, his organ. Is it not clear that fact and fancy are mixed and twisted in Garvey's mind?

A paranoiac is unduly suspicious. He suffers from the delusion of persecution. He is always looking for treachery. He imagines someone is always trying to harm him.

Garvey's speeches are shot through with statements showing that the above is his frame of mind. He is continually talking of conspiracies and plots. His delusion is that he is the victim of persecution.

## Simple essay style

Below is a sample exam question. Use your own knowledge and the information on the opposite page to produce a plan for this question. Choose four general points, and provide three pieces of specific information to support each general point. Once you have planned your essay, write the introduction and conclusion for the essay. The introduction should list the points to be discussed in the essay. The conclusion should summarise the key points and justify which point was the most important.

> How far did cultural changes in the 1920s reflect the tensions in US society?

# Popular entertainment

The 1920s saw significant changes in popular entertainment. It was an age of 'fads' such as new dances associated with jazz, new games such as Mah-Jong and the development of cinema, radio and mass spectator sports, all fuelled by widespread advertising and sponsorship. The decade was called 'The Roaring Twenties'.

## Radio

Radio ownership grew dramatically with the electrification process across the USA and so did radio coverage. By 1922 there were 500 local stations with the first national network, NBC, set up in 1926. It allowed people all over the USA to link up for significant events, which were broadcast nationally – in 1927, for example, 50 million people listened to the boxing match between heavyweights Gene Tunney and Jack Dempsey.

Radio sales grew from $60 million in 1923 to $842 million by 1929. Programmes were sponsored by advertisers knowing an audience could get hooked on exciting serials or comedy programmes such as *Amos 'n' Andy*, with an audience rising to as many as 40 million. Overwhelmingly, the focus of radio was on entertainment rather than education. This is what most people wanted.

## Cinema

Cinema was even more popular, with stars such as Mary Pickford and Charlie Chaplin becoming household names. By the 1920s the cinema industry based in Hollywood was the fourth largest in the USA in terms of capitalist investment and employed more people than either Ford or General Motors.

Movies, which were initially silent, offered an escape from the everyday world where viewers could dream of being like their heroes on screen. Many cinemas resembled palaces, plush and glamorous, and held audiences of hundreds. In any one day there could be more than 10 million people watching films at 20,000 cinemas. The advent of sound in 1927 made them even more popular.

## Moral corruption

The widespread fascination with cinema, particularly among the young, led to fears of moral corruption among more conservative voices. There were concerns not only in terms of audiences being closeted together in the dark but also what messages the films might convey. Scandals among stars, such as accusations of severe sexual misconduct against the comic actor Roscoe 'Fatty' Arbuckle in 1926, led to the appointment of Will Hays as a censor to ensure film content remained 'clean' and 'wholesome'.

## Sport

The 1920s was also an age of mass spectator sport. Many sports personalities became millionaires, often through sponsorship. It was estimated that the boxer Jack Dempsey made $10 million over the course of his career, while baseball star **Babe Ruth** made over $800,000 just from playing.

## Baseball

Baseball became particularly popular due to the emergence of supremely talented players during the decade, notably Babe Ruth and Lou Gehrig. Massive stadia were built such as the West Side Grounds in Chicago and radio regularly covered matches for those who could not attend. However, the sport was strictly racially segregated.

## Negro National Baseball League

Baseball was popular among black and white Americans. The Negro National Baseball league was formed in 1920 to accommodate black American players and spectators. The high point of the season, the East-West All-star game attracted crowds of over 30,000. Black American Leagues were among the most profitable black-American owned businesses.

## Spot the inference

High-level answers avoid excessive summarising or paraphrasing the sources. Instead they make inferences from the sources, as well as analysing their value in terms of their context.

Below are a source and a series of statements. Read the source and decide which of the statements:

- makes inferences from the source (I)
- paraphrases the source (P)
- summarise the source (S)
- cannot be justified from the source (X)

Fill in the boxes below with either I, P, S, or X: ☐

- Some high school teachers believe the movies are a powerful factor in helping young people to grow up in society. ☐
- One working-class mother sends her daughter to learn about life from the movies. ☐
- The movies teach young people about real life. ☐
- The judge would disagree with the view of the mother in that the movies present a 'good, safe' means of teaching her daughter about life. ☐
- Many people believe the movies lead to immoral behaviour. ☐

## SOURCE 1

From Robert and Helen Lynd, 'Inventions Remaking Leisure', in *Middletown, A Study in American Culture*, published in 1929. The Lynds were sociologists who extensively studied the lives of ordinary Americans living in the town of Muncie, Indiana, which they referred to as 'Middletown'.

Actual changes of habits resulting from week after week of witnessing these films can be inferred. Young Middletown is finding discussion of problems of mating in the new agency that boasts in large illustrated advertisements, 'Girls! You will learn how to handle 'em!' and 'Is it true marriage kills love?' If you want to know what love really means, its exquisite torture, its overwhelming raptures, see -

Some high school teachers are convinced that the movies are a powerful factor in bringing about the 'early sophistication' of the young and the relaxing of social taboos. One working class mother frankly welcomes the movies as an aid in child rearing, saying, 'I send my daughter because a girl has to learn the ways of the world somehow and the movies are a good, safe way.' The judge of the juvenile court lists the movies as one of the 'big four' causes of local juvenile delinquency, believing that the disregard of group mores by the young is definitely related to the witnessing week after week of fictional sequences that habitually link the taking of long chances and the happy ending.

## Simple essay style

Below is a sample AS exam question. Use your own knowledge and the information on the previous and opposite page to produce a plan for this question. Choose four general points, and provide three pieces of specific information to support each general point. Once you have planned your essay, write the introduction and conclusion for the essay. The introduction should list the points to be discussed in the essay. The conclusion should summarise the key points and justify which point was the most important.

How far did popular culture change during the 1920s?

# Exam focus

On pages 26–28 are sample exam answers to the questions on these two pages. Read the answers and the comments around them.

Why is Source 1 valuable to the historian for an enquiry into the extent of the 'Red Scare' in 1920? Explain your answer using the source, the information given about it and your own knowledge of the historical context. **AS**

How far could the historian make use of Sources 1 and 2 together to investigate the impact of the Red Scare of 1920 on fears of revolution in the USA? Explain your answer, using both sources, the information given about them and your own knowledge of the historical context.

## SOURCE 1

From 'The Case Against the Reds', written by A Mitchell Palmer in the periodical *The Forum* in February 1920. Palmer is summarising the threat presented by Communists and other radical left-wing groups and the government response.

The nationality of most of the alien Reds is Russian and German. There is almost no other nationality represented among them. It has been impossible in so short a space to review the entire menace of the internal revolution in this country as I know it, but this may serve to arouse the American citizen to its reality, its danger and the great need of united effort to stamp it out, under our feet if needs be. It is being done. The Department of Justice will pursue the attack of these 'Reds' upon the government of the United States with vigilance and no alien advocating the overthrow of existing law and order in this country shall escape arrest and prompt deportation.

It is my belief that while they have stirred discontent in our midst, while they have caused irritating strikes and while they have infected our social ideas with the disease of their own minds and their unclean morals, we can get rid of them, and not until we have done so shall we have removed the menace of Bolshevism for good.

## SOURCE 2

From *Only Yesterday: An Informal History of the 1920s*, written by Frederick Lewis Allen, published in 1931. Allen was a well-respected and objective journalist who always strove for a balanced view.

William J Burns put the number of resident Communists at 422,000 and S Stanward Menkin of the National Security League made it 600,000 – figures at least ten times as large as those of Watkins. Dwight Braman, president of the Allied Patriotic Societies told Governor Smith of New York that the reds were holding 10,000 meetings in the country every week, and that 350 radical newspapers had been established in the preceding six months.

But not only the Communists were dangerous; they had, it seemed, well disguised or unwitting allies in more respectable circles. The Russian Famine Fund committee, according to Ralph Eastley of the National Civic Federation included sixty pronounced Communist sympathisers... There was hardly a liberal civic organisation in the land at which the protectors of the nation did not bid the citizenry to shudder.

The effect of these admonitions was oppressive. The fear of the radicals was accompanied and followed by a fear of being thought radical... a liberal journalist visiting a formerly outspoken Hoosier [name for resident of the state of Indiana] in his office was not permitted to talk politics until his frightened host had closed and locked the door and closed the window.

Below is the answer to the AS Level question on Source 1.

The source is valuable for an enquiry into the extent of the Red Scare in the USA, in the sense that it was written by Mitchell Palmer, the Attorney General or chief law enforcement officer who was in large part responsible for unleashing the scare. Its purpose is both to alert people to the extent of the Red Scare and reassure them that the Justice department have the situation under control – and there to a certain extent lies a flaw in the argument.

> Purpose of source explained.

It was written at a time when there was real fear of revolution in the USA in the lines of the Bolshevik revolution in Russia and the Spartacist insurrections in Germany.

> Context of source explained.

We note therefore that Palmer specifically mentioned most of the revolutionaries in the USA as coming from those two countries to enhance people's fears – although the Red Scare was in fact targeted both at home-spun revolutionaries and recent arrivals, noticeably from southern and eastern Europe.

> Critical engagement with source.

The source is further useful as evidence of how Palmer tried to reassure people that the Justice Department was in control of the situation, arresting and deporting suspected revolutionary aliens. In fact, the Palmer Raids of January 1920 led to 6,000 arrests, the vast majority of whom were released in the absence of any evidence against them.

> Using own knowledge to support criticism of source content.

The source is also useful in how it illustrates the contradiction in Palmer's thinking. On the one hand, the language emphasises the scale of the crisis, 'infecting' US values with the 'diseases of their minds' while on the other reassuring them with the work of the Justice department, but also using phrases, such as 'irritating strikes', which suggest the activities of revolutionaries, while inconvenient, do not in fact threaten the fabric of the USA. While Palmer seeks to emphasise the threat, he does not want to suggest that his Department has lost control of the situation.

> Using language and tone to show the flaw in the argument.

However, while Palmer emphasises the extent of the threat, this is largely asserted. He does not offer much evidence to support his assertion. He is anxious to say who the revolutionaries are and what his department is doing about them – but while this in itself would imply a threat to the USA and while it no doubt fuelled fears among the public of a Red Scare, it still did not give hard evidence about how real in concrete terms the scare actually was.

Overall, then, the source is useful in showing the Red Scare from the perspective of one who was charged to address it, but also suggestive that despite the dramatic words, the Red Scare may not be so real after all – Palmer asserts what it was but offers in this extract little evidence of how widespread or threatening it actually was.

> Overall judgement on utility, with valid inference based on hidden meaning.

**This response has a strong focus upon the question and gives three clear reasons why the source is useful for the enquiry. Passages from the source, a consideration of the source's context and the nature, origin and purpose of the source are used to make valid inferences.**

### Consolidation (sources)

This answer demands a combination of argument, own knowledge and reference to sources. Colour code each of these three components.

Below is the answer to the A Level question on page 26.

Both sources are useful in part in investigating the impact of the Red Scare on revolutionary fears in that each is given from a different perspective, concluding with a different judgement so the historian can see that there is a range of views about the impact of the Red Scare. The first source is written by Mitchell Palmer, the Attorney General responsible for instigating the response to the Red Scare, while the second is a more reasoned account from an objective journalist of the impact from the perspective of ten years' hence. It may have been in Palmer's interests to exaggerate the extent of the scare, while the journalist is attempting to be impartial in his reflection of the impact of the scare.

**Introduction is well focused on the question and summarises the nature of each source.**

As the person charged with the ending of the Red Scare it would be in the interests of Palmer in Source 1 to emphasise the seriousness of the Red Scare in terms of its threat of revolution in order to reassure people that the Justice Department was combating it effectively, but never minimising the scale of the threat. This judgement on its impact may therefore be unreliable in terms of accuracy. Source 2 on the other hand is more measured. While Allen begins with evidence of the extent of the belief in fears of revolution, he implies that it was nevertheless exaggerated and offers evidence of contrasting views. In this context, while his initial comments may appear to support the assertions of Palmer in Source 1, he goes on to offer the contrasting views of Professor Watkins and then considers the impact of the Scare on the very USA values, for example of free speech, which Palmer was purporting to defend.

**Purpose of source discussed.**

In terms of the arguments deployed, the first source is more dramatic – Reds 'have infected our social ideas with the disease of their own minds' – while the second is more reasoned, considering the impact in terms of the oppressiveness of fear and suspicion and how one formerly outspoken person – presumably offered as one example of many – was afraid to speak openly. In effect, Palmer is saying that Communism and Anarchy – and by implication the Red Scare – pose a significant threat to American values, while Allen is inclined to view the impact as more about fear on the part of Americans and that their liberal views may be misconstrued as radical. Palmer argues that the Justice Department activities are necessary, while Allen implies the results of suspicions, such as attacks on civic societies of all kinds, was oppression and fear.

**Contrast of language to discuss tone of each source.**

**Summary of sources' content.**

In terms of provenance, Palmer is clearly biased. As Attorney General or the principal law enforcement officer in the USA he could hardly be expected to negate the Red Scare. He would have to emphasise the threat in order to praise the Justice Department's response, which must be seen as necessary and not an over-reaction. Allen, as a journalist trying to interpret the events ten years later, has no such qualms. However, we should note that Palmer was writing at the time. Unlike Allen, he did not have the luxury of hindsight. If he genuinely believed in the reality of the Red Scare, he would be extremely negligent in not placing the might of the law enforcement powers of the USA to combat it.

Neither source really discusses in the extracts the nature of the Red Scare itself. However, with 4 million workers on strike at specific times in 1919, crimes of robbery and violence, and political assassinations (including an attempt on Palmer himself) the scare should not be minimised. Palmer undoubtedly was reflecting common concerns at the time about the threat of revolution in the USA. Allen acknowledges these fears as being genuinely felt, at the time, although he is more at pains to discuss their consequences on US values. While Palmer emphasises the fears of Communist revolution, Allen focuses on the effects of such fears on issues such as free speech and openness in discussing ideas.

**Valid use of context.**

Allen does however suggest the unpleasant nature of the threat. The fears that Communists have infiltrated seemingly respectable organisations exacerbates the fears in the sense that they are not in the open and one doesn't know whom to trust – thus enhancing the suspicions, which would lead to the oppression and fear he outlined.

**Subtle inference.**

Both sources are limited by the lack of concrete evidence in support. Both make claims but often offer little information to back them up. Allen, for example, gives the example of only one man who is afraid to talk. While this example may indeed be expected to stand for many, in itself it cannot do so. Palmer meanwhile asserts the significance of the threat, but neither in the extracts as they stand offer concrete evidence in support. Palmer asserts the impact of the Red Scare is the diligence of the Justice Department. Allen asserts it is oppression and fear. However, while Palmer does not in fact examine the threat of the Red Scare on the people of the USA, Allen does, showing how the fears of Revolution can impact on their lives. Palmer tells the reader the threat is real and his department is combating it: Allen focuses more on the impact of this.

**Distinguishes between claims and information.**

**Discussing limitations of each source.**

Both sources are partly useful to an historian investigating the impact of the Red Scare on fears of revolution. They offer differing views because they come from different perspectives at different times, with Allen having the benefit of perspective to ostensibly minimise the threat. However, both lack evidence in support and tend to assert rather than argue – this limits their value in terms of authoritativeness, but might enhance it in terms of how Americans viewed the impact of the Red Scare at the time and shortly afterwards.

**Conclusion summarises well and makes valid judgement as to source utility.**

This response is clearly a high Level 5. It interrogates the source well to make valid inferences, including hidden meanings as, for example, where Allen might unwittingly have corroborated Palmer's assertions. It uses context to support points made and distinguishes between opinion and information. An overall judgement is supported by valid criteria, showing how much weight the sources can bear.

**Consolidation (sources)**

It is useful to analyse sample answers such as this by colour coding 'similarity', 'difference', 'own knowledge' and 'provenance'. This helps to recognise the relationship between each component part of the answer, and gives ideas on how such answers can be constructed.

# 2 Depression and New Deal, 1933–38

## The spread of the Depression, 1929–32

REVISED

Between 1929 and 1932, economic depression spread throughout the USA. Although the signs of economic problems had been evident throughout the 1920s (see page 10), after the Wall Street Crash of 1929 the economy seemed to collapse. This was the period of the **Great Depression**. Unemployment soared, **Gross National Product (GNP)** collapsed, and the banking system came dangerously close to meltdown. However, some regions and some industries escaped the worst effects of the Depression.

### Growth of unemployment

Unemployment grew from 1,550,000 or 3.14 per cent of the labour force in 1929 to 12,830,000 or 24.75 per cent by 1933.

The national wage bill in 1932 was only 40 per cent of the 1929 figure. However, unemployment was not spread evenly across the country: by 1933 the Ohio city of Toledo faced 80 per cent unemployment, while Kilgore, Texas had comparatively little unemployment due to a temporary oil boom. Some industries, such as cigarette and light bulb manufacture, remained relatively immune to the Depression.

### Collapse of Gross Domestic Product

National wealth as defined in terms of **Gross Domestic Product (GDP)** showed a significant decline during the Depression. It fell, for example, from $103.8 billion in 1929 to $56.2 billion by 1932.

In real terms, this meant the national growth rate went into a sharp decline from an annual rate of 6.7 per cent in 1929 to –14.7 per cent in 1932.

### Problems with credit and banking

There were significant problems with credit and banking, with credit in particular being rarely available. The USA became a land of cash transactions. The Stock Exchange remained depressed despite occasional rallies. Over 10,000 banks failed between 1929 and 1932.

## Effects on individual industries

While most industries and areas were affected by the Depression, individuals who did keep their jobs tended to be better off as wages rose. General price levels fell by 25 per cent during the early 1930s. However, the 1930s was also a period of business innovation with the introduction of air conditioning, airline travel and supermarkets. While the country as a whole remained in the grip of depression, it should not be forgotten that pockets of prosperity remained.

### Modern industries

Some more modern industries such as air conditioning providers escaped the worst effects. One notable industry to do well was aviation, which saw the first cross-continent flights and an increase in airline passengers from 474,000 in 1932 to 1,178,858 by 1938.

### Older industries

- In the construction industry the number of newly built residential units fell 82 per cent between 1929 and 1932. The value of construction contracts fell from $6.6 billion in 1929 to $1.3 billion three years later.
- The workforce in the coal industry fell by 300,000 between 1929 and 1932.
- Iron and steel production fell by 59 per cent between 1929 and 1932 and by 1932 the US Steel Corporation's workforce was entirely part time.
- Car sales fell from 4,455,178 in 1929 to 1,103,557 four years later and one car manufacturing firm, Willis-Overland, dismissed all but 3,000 of their 25,000 strong workforce.

### Geographical impact

Overall the areas that suffered the most were the agricultural South and the traditional industrial areas of the North; areas that had been under economic pressure before the onset of Depression.

## Spectrum of importance

Below are a sample AS exam question and a list of general points, which could be used to answer the question. Use your own knowledge and the information on the opposite page to reach a judgement about the importance of these general points to the question posed. Write numbers on the spectrum below to indicate their relative importance. Having done this, write a brief justification of your placement, explaining why some of these factors are more important than others. The resulting diagram could form the basis of an essay plan.

How widespread was the Depression in the USA in the early 1930s?

1 Unemployment

2 GDP

3 Centres of traditional industries

4 Iron and steel production

5 Problems with banking

6 New Industries

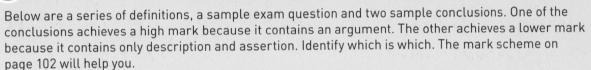

Least important          Most important

## Identify an argument

Below are a series of definitions, a sample exam question and two sample conclusions. One of the conclusions achieves a high mark because it contains an argument. The other achieves a lower mark because it contains only description and assertion. Identify which is which. The mark scheme on page 102 will help you.

- Description: a detailed account.
- Assertion: a statement of fact or an opinion which is not supported by a reason.
- Reason: a statement which explains or justifies something.
- Argument: an assertion justified with a reason.

'The economic impact of the Depression on the USA was deeply uneven.' How far do you agree with this statement?

> The Depression was widespread across the USA. In 1933 Gross National Product (GNP) was half that of 1929, unemployment stood at 25 per cent of the workforce and the banking system was in trouble. The city of Toledo faced 80 per cent unemployment. The workforce in the coal industry fell by 300,000. Iron and steel production fell by 59 per cent and by 1932 car sales fell from 4,455,178 in 1929 to 1,103,557 four years later. One car manufacturing firm, Willis-Overland, dismissed all but 3,000 of their 25,000-strong workforce. Stocks prices remained low — in December 1932 the Wall Street index stood at 84.81. However, it was not even. Some newer industries such as aviation did well, while some areas remained prosperous for much of the period, for example, oil towns such as Kilgore in Texas.

> While the impact and extent of the Depression was clearly devastating, it was not all-embracing in its distribution, and some industries and areas did escape its worst effects. New industries such as aviation prospered during the Depression years — the number of passengers grew from 474,000 in 1932 to 1,178,858 by 1938. The impact of the Depression also varied over time. The Texas oil town of Kilgore, for example, enjoyed a temporary boom as new stocks were discovered. However, while there were pockets of prosperity, the overall picture was more one of economic collapse, with 25 per cent unemployment in 1932 and Northeastern centres of traditional industries such as iron and steel, where the workforce shrank by 300,000, being particularly badly affected.

# The human impact of the Depression

The human cost of the Depression was enormous. The USA lacked an infrastructure to deal with mass employment. There was, for example, no federal aid and charities could not cope. The prevailing philosophy had been that the unemployed were to blame for their plight and they could find work with determination and effort. While the Depression showed that this was not the case, there were few ideas to replace it.

## Workers and hoboes

Many people facing unemployment were forced to sell their possessions, and then rely on charities. However, charities were under tremendous pressures and the demands on them grew as their funds dried up. Many unemployed became **hoboes**, moving across the country, often stowing away on freight trains in search of work – by 1932 it was estimated that there were over 1 million itinerant workers without regular or fixed employment. Many areas passed laws against them and railroads employed guards to throw them off trains.

## Homelessness and the Hoovervilles

Many Americans who lost their homes as a result of becoming unemployed in the Depression moved to the outskirts of urban areas. They built homes of tin, wood and cardboard, which became known as **Hoovervilles**. President **Hoover** was blamed for the lack of support and relief, and the sarcastic name for the dwellings soon caught on. Hoovervilles had few facilities and were usually insanitary and squalid. It has been estimated that at their peak, several hundred thousand people across the USA lived in these **shanty towns**.

There were other terms, heavy with irony, which used Hoover's name. For example, old newspapers, which homeless people wrapped themselves up in to keep warm, were dubbed 'Hoover blankets'.

## Families

The strain on families led to a fall in marriages from 1.23 million in 1929 to 982,000 by 1932, with a concomitant fall in the birth rate. Suicide rates increased from 14 per 10,000 in 1929 to 17.4 by 1932 – and the majority of elderly people with few support mechanisms were living below the poverty line.

## Farmers

Farm prices collapsed as demand fell. Wheat rotted in the fields because farmers could not afford to harvest it. Many farmers saw their mortgages foreclosed, which meant that their properties were confiscated when they could not afford to repay the mortgage loan. **Sharecroppers** were the worst affected. As their income reduced they could not meet the payments – and were evicted.

## Ethnic minorities

The Depression generally affected people of colour to a much greater extent than white Americans.
- Black Americans were four to six times more likely to be unemployed than their white counterparts, and increasingly low-paid jobs reserved for them were offered to whites.
- Native Americans had largely been living in poverty on their reservations and the Depression made it even more difficult for them to find work away from them.
- Around 400,000 Hispanic Americans were deported to Latin America even if they had had lived in the USA all their lives.

## Women

Women generally faced dismissal before their male colleagues. Additionally, half the 48 states had laws banning the employment of married women. This meant women who may have been economically independent during the 1920s became dependent again on husbands or family.

## The extent of relief

Before 1932 no state had any system of unemployment insurance and only 11 operated any form of pension scheme – with a total outlay of only $220,000 aiding a mere 1,000 people in total. There were few private pension schemes and they catered for the relatively well off.

## Gangsterism

The Depression led to a rise in crime, particularly among outlaw gangs in the Southwest. These often attained '**Robin Hood**' status, gaining a reputation for robbing banks, which were blamed for evicting farmers. However, they rarely shared their loot and preferred to rob stores and gas stations, because they were easier targets than banks.

Many of these gangs were violent and preyed on the very people who saw them as heroes. The Clyde Barrow gang – Bonnie and Clyde – once shot a store clerk in order to steal a total of $28. Most met violent deaths: Bonnie and Clyde were shot and killed in an ambush in Louisiana in May 1934, while John Dillinger – Public Enemy Number One – was killed in an **FBI** trap the following July.

## Highlighting integration

Below are a sample A Level Section A question and two paragraphs written in answer to this question. Read the question and the two answers, as well as the sources. Then, using a highlighter, highlight examples of integration – where sources are used together.

Tip: Integration of the sources is a useful technique in answering a question - but make sure the integration is relevant to the question.

How far could the historian make use of Sources 1 and 2 together to investigate attitudes to hoboes in the early 1930s?

Source 1 is useful as it shows hoboes weren't just single young men, but sometimes whole families took to the road. However, Albright was interviewed forty years after the events she is describing so her memory could be unreliable. Source 2 similarly is recounted many years after the events it describes. It is useful for showing hostile attitudes and also the shame Banks felt in being unemployed. However, it is only one person's view so may not be typical.

Both sources are partially useful in investigating attitudes to hoboes. Both are part of different oral history projects so both may have the same problems of reliability in that the respondents are describing events of many years previously and reliant on memory.

## SOURCE 1

Interview with Lora Albright, a rancher's wife about her experiences during the Depression undertaken by the Latah County Historical Society in 1976.

... never refused to feed anybody that came to my door and asked. And Raleigh (her husband) sometimes felt that if they were young and healthy that they should do something to help earn it. And there was always things on the ranch from chopping wood to hoeing that they could do. And one day there was a family, a young man, I suppose he was in his middle thirties, because there was four children that were walking, and the wife was carrying a baby, which would be five children, and they had to get to Troy, Idaho. And they had come up through Southern Idaho, just catching rides just anyway that they could. And they had no money when they got here, and that man was carrying what clothes they had. He must have had two hundred pounds on his back, I was aghast; and they were trying to get Troy to her uncle's, as I understood it, and they had lost a business down in the middle part of the state there. Well, what could you do but bring them in?

## SOURCE 2

From the memories of Louis Banks, a former hobo in Studs Terkel, *Hard Times*, published in 1970. Terkel interviewed hundreds of people about their lives during the Depression. Banks, an ex-prizefighter and chef eventually escaped the Depression by joining the army.

And then I saw a railroad police, a white police... He shoots you off all trains. We came out of Lima, Ohio... Lima Slim would kill you if he catch you on any train. He would shoot you off, he wouldn't ask you to get off.

I was in chain gangs and had been in jail all over the country. I was in a chain gang in Georgia. I had to pick cotton for four months, for just hoboin' on a train.

A man had to be on the road. He had to leave his wife, had to leave his mother, his family just to try to get money to live on. But he think: my dear mother, tryin' to send her money, tryin' to send her money, worryin' how she's starvin'.

The shame I was feelin'. I walked out because I didn't have a job. I said, 'I'm goin' out in the world and get me a job.' And God help me, I couldn't get anything. I wouldn't let them see me all dirty and ragged and I haven't shaved. I wouldn't send em no picture.

I'd write: 'Dear mother, I'm doin' wonderful and wish you're all fine.'

# The presidency of Herbert Hoover, 1929–33

President Hoover recognised the scale of the Depression but believed people should help themselves. His response to the Depression was a mixture of **voluntarism** and indirect aid through loans to industry and states. Although he was to intervene more than any other president, the measures he took were inadequate to address the scale of the Depression and he could not countenance direct government relief.

## Hoover – background and beliefs

Hoover was a self-made man who had enjoyed a successful career as an engineer and businessman, before turning to politics. He had served as Secretary of Commerce during the 1920s, when he was generally regarded as being one of the architects of prosperity. He was associated with efficiency and good governance.

Although he had humanitarian views – he had been a tireless organiser of relief work during the First World War – Hoover had a view of the limited role of government, which fundamentally he could not alter.

### 'American individualism'

Hoover's beliefs were spelled out in a 1922 book *American Individualism*, which reflected earlier ideas that were common in the USA, such as **rugged individualism**. Broadly, he believed that everyone with the right opportunities could become as successful as he had. He believed passionately that the Government should give people the ability to solve problems by themselves but should not get directly involved.

## Attempts to combat the Depression

Hoover worked tirelessly to combat the Depression. Publically, the President had to appear optimistic as to how far the economy was recovering. This suggested to many that he was out of touch with reality. For example, Hoover's announcement to the press that unemployment was falling caused resentment among the millions of jobless.

Hoover blamed world economic conditions for the Depression, particularly the effects of the First World War, which led to lack of trust between countries. International trade had collapsed and countries could not meet their economic responsibilities. He believed, for example, the Depression had spread to the USA largely as a result of countries not being able to repay their loans to USA banks.

Many of Hoover's earlier measures therefore were designed to insulate the USA from international economic problems – for example, through **protection**.

## International trade

### The Smoot–Hawley tariff

Hoover's initial reaction was to protect US industry from foreign competition. In July 1930, against the advice of many economists, he signed the Smoot–Hawley tariff, which had been introduced in Congress. It was the highest tariff in US history with 40 per cent on both industrial and agricultural imports. The result was a devastating fall in international trade of $1.2 billion by 1931. The tariff harmed both US industrialists whose foreign clients could no longer afford to buy US goods and US farmers who needed to sell their huge surpluses abroad.

Having passed this to protect US commerce, however, Hoover also sought in part to remedy its impact and help European economies recover by the repudiation of war debts.

### Repudiation of war debts

As the Depression spread throughout the world, Hoover announced in June 1931 that the USA would postpone the collection of **war debts** for 18 months. This was designed to help countries begin to trade again – although it did nothing to solve the problems caused by the Smoot–Hawley tariff and in any event most countries remained too poor to see any resurgence in international trade.

## Explain the difference  **a**

The following sources give different accounts of the economic problems facing the USA in 1929. List the ways in which the sources differ. Explain the differences between the sources using the provenance of the sources, and the historical context. The provenance appears at the top of the source. Make sure you stay focused on the differences that are relevant to the A Level question below.

How far could the historian make use of Sources 1 and 2 to investigate the extent of the economic problems facing the USA after 1929?

Explain your answer, using both sources, the information given about them and your own knowledge of the historical context.

### SOURCE 1

Extract from a news conference by President Herbert Hoover, 25 October 1929.

The fundamental business of the country, that is, production and distribution of commodities, is on a very sound and prosperous basis. The best evidence is that although production and consumption are at a very high level, the average price of these commodities, taken as whole, have shown no increase in the whole of the last twelve months and there has been no appreciable increase in the stock of manufactured goods. Therefore, there has been no speculation in commodities. There has been a tendency for wage increases, and output per worker has increased, all of which indicate a very healthy situation.

The construction and building materials industries have been somewhat affected by the high interest rates induced by New York speculation, and there is some seasonal decrease in two or three other industries, but these movements are of secondary character when they are considered in the light of the whole situation.

### SOURCE 2

Extract from a speech given by Frances Perkins in 1982. Perkins was senior official in Franklin Delano Roosevelt's administration who had been his Labor Commissioner while he was Governor of New York during the onset of the Depression. Perkins' work here brought her into daily contact with the impact of the Depression on individuals.

Since 1929 we had experienced the short, sudden drop of everything. The total economy had gone to pieces; just shook to pieces under us, beginning, of course, with the stock market crash. A banking crisis followed it. A manufacturing crisis followed it. Everybody felt it. In less than a year it was a terror.

People were so alarmed that all through the rest of 1929, 1930 and 1931, the specter of unemployment – of starvation, of hunger, of the wondering boys, of the broken homes, of the families separated while everybody went out to look for work – stalked everywhere. The unpaid rent, the eviction notices, the furniture and bedding on the sidewalk, the old lady weeping over it, the children crying, the father out looking for a truck to move their belongings himself to his sister's flat or some relative's already overcrowded tenement, or just sitting there bewilderingly, waiting for some charity office to come and move him somewhere.

## Simple essay style

Below is a sample exam question. Use your own knowledge and the information on the opposite page to produce a plan for this question. Choose four general points, and provide three pieces of specific information to support each general point. Once you have planned your essay, write the introduction and conclusion for the essay. The introduction should list the points to be discussed in the essay. The conclusion should summarise the key points and justify which point was the most important.

How accurate is it to say that Hoover's initial responses to the Great Depression reflected his belief that world economic conditions were the principal cause?

# Hoover's response to the Depression, 1929–33

Although Hoover intervened in the economy more than any other president, his measures were insufficient to address the scale of the Depression.

## Government measures

While he could not consent to direct government relief in the form, for example, of welfare, Hoover nevertheless intervened more than any other president to try to end the Depression.

### Unemployment Relief

Hoover secured $500,000 from **Congress** in 1932 to help charities and relief agencies, and set up the President's Emergency Relief Committee to help them co-ordinate their efforts. However, the measures were inadequate. It was generally agreed that direct government relief was necessary. Hoover refused this even when a severe drought saw near starvation conditions in the South in 1930–31. Congress, in fact, allocated only $47 million to alleviate distress here and even that was in the form of loans, which had to be repaid.

### Federal Home Loan Bank Act

This measure, passed in June 1932, was intended to save mortgages by making credit easier, thereby avoiding evictions. Federal Loan banks were set up to help provide loan associations provide mortgages. However, these loans were no more than 50 per cent of the value of the property, and therefore often inadequate in preventing homes being repossessed due to non-payment of mortgages.

### The Reconstruction Finance Corporation 1932

The Reconstruction Finance Corporation (RFC) was established in July 1932 to lend up to $2 billion to banks, railroads and other financial institutions in trouble. Its aim was to restore confidence, particularly in the financial system. However, critics said most of the monies went to the largest institutions – indeed 50 per cent of the loans went to the seven largest banks. The Central Republican National Bank and Trust Company alone received $90 million – almost as much as it held in total deposits at the time.

The Government argued that it made sense to help the largest firms remain solvent as they were the biggest employers. Many felt, however, that the RFC helped powerful institutions but did nothing for the people who really needed help – the unemployed and dispossessed. It was pressure from these voices that was finally influential in the provision of some form of relief.

### Emergency Relief and Construction Act 1932

The Emergency Relief and Construction Act was set up in the summer of 1932 and authorised the RFC to lend up to $1.5 billion to states to finance public works, which could provide employment. However, to be eligible states had to be bankrupt and the projects would have to generate enough revenue to pay off the loans.

### The Bonus Army

In 1932 the **Bonus Army** of Great War veterans descended on Washington to demand their **war pensions** early. They were moved on forcibly by the military amid scenes of brutality for which Hoover again was blamed.

While some conservative critics said Hoover was intervening too much and the Depression would right itself if left alone, most felt he had not done enough and would not be voting for him in the 1932 presidential election.

**Add the context**

Below is a sample A Level exam question with the accompanying sources. Having read the question and the sources, complete the following activity.

> How far could the historian make use of Sources 1 and 2 together to investigate reactions to the Bonus Marchers of 1932 in relation to fears of lawlessness and political unrest?

First, look for aspects of the source that refer to the events and concerns that were going on around the time that the source was written. Underline the key phrases and write a brief description of the context in the margin next to the source. Draw an arrow from the key phrase to the context. Try to find three key phrases in each source.

## SOURCE 1

From a public statement about the Bonus Marchers given by President Hoover on 29 July 1932. The president was justifying the action taken against the Bonus Marchers.

The president said:

A challenge to the authority of the United States Government has been met, swiftly and firmly.

After months of patient indulgence, the Government met overt lawlessness as it always must be met if the cherished processes of self-government are to be preserved. We cannot tolerate the abuse of constitutional rights by those who would destroy all government, no matter who they may be. Government cannot be coerced by mob rule.

The Department of Justice is pressing its investigation into the violence which forced the call for Army detachments, and it is my sincere hope that those agitators who inspired yesterday's attack upon the Federal authority may be brought speedily to trial in the civil courts. There can be no safe harbor in the United States of America for violence.

Order and civil tranquillity are the first requisites in the great task of economic reconstruction to which our whole people now are devoting their heroic and noble energies. This national effort must not be retarded in even the slightest degree by organized lawlessness. The first obligation of my office is to uphold and defend the Constitution and the authority of the law. This I propose always to do.

## SOURCE 2

From Malcolm Cowley, *The Dream of Golden Mountains,* published in 1934. Cowley was an important literary figure whose autobiography *The Dream of Golden Mountains* reflected his left-wing views.

A few weeks later there was more talk of revolution when the Bonus Expeditionary Force descended on Washington. The BEF was a tattered army consisting of veterans from every state in the Union; most of them were old-stock Americans from smaller industrial cities where relief had broken down. All unemployed in 1932, all living on the edge of hunger, they remembered that the government had made them a promise for the future. It was embodied in a law that Congress had passed some years before, providing 'adjusted compensation certificates' for those who had served in the Great War; the certificates were to be redeemed in dollars, but not until 1945... They organized themselves by states and companies and chose a commander named Walter W. Waters, an ex-sergeant from Portland, Oregon, who promptly acquired an aide-de-camp and a pair of highly polished leather puttees. Meanwhile the veterans were listening to speakers of all political complexions, as the Russian soldiers had done in 1917. Many radicals and some conservatives thought that the Bonus Army was creating a revolutionary situation of an almost classical type.

# Roosevelt and the First New Deal, 1933–35

Franklin Delano Roosevelt was elected president in 1932. He promised a '**New Deal**' to restore faith in the US economy through the goals of relief, recovery and reform. However, there was no specific blueprint about how this would be achieved and Roosevelt was a **fiscal conservative** committed to a balanced budget. Roosevelt was charismatic, appealing to people via '**fireside chats**' on the radio and engendering confidence in his policies. 'The only thing we have to fear', he once said, 'is fear itself' by which he meant that Americans could overcome the Depression by boldness and resolution, with his government leading the way.

## The Hundred Days

The first hundred days of Roosevelt's presidency saw more legislation than at any previous time in US history. It transformed both the role of the US Government and people's expectations of it in terms of its activities. In particular, emergency legislation was passed and '**alphabet agencies**' were set up to deal with the problems of the Depression.

## Emergency relief

The Federal Emergency Relief Administration (FERA) was set up in May 1933. It was given $500 million to divide equally among states to provide relief for the unemployed. Half was given directly by FERA to the states and half kept back, to give them $1 for every $3 of their own funds they spent on relief. Some states refused to comply.

Roosevelt hoped to make the emergency relief measures self-financing and they were often started with loans. It was hoped these would be repaid, for example, as public works projects went into profit.

The funding was insufficient for the scale of the problem – but it set a precedent as the first example of direct federal government relief.

## Alphabet agencies

Sixteen alphabet agencies were set up to deal with specific issues relating to recovery from the Depression and relief for those affected by it.

## Help for farmers

Agricultural problems such as overproduction were dealt with by the Agricultural Adjustment Agency (AAA), which paid farmers to produce less. It was hoped this would solve the problems of overproduction and see prices rise as a result of reduced output. Cotton, for example, saw prices rise from 6.5 to 10 cents per pound as 10.5 million acres of cotton fields were taken out of production. More contentious was the slaughter of 6 million piglets to enable the price of pork to rise.

On the surface the agency was successful in that prices of produce affected rose. Total farm income rose from $4.5 billion in 1932 to $6.9 billion two years later. However, it was also to cause problems later (see page 56).

## Help for industry

The National Industry Recovery Act (NIRA) set up the National Recovery Administration (NRA) to facilitate industrial recovery. Firms were encouraged to agree to codes establishing:
- working conditions
- product standards.

## Public works

The second part of the NRA was the Public Works Administration, funded with $3.3 billion with the aim of **pump-priming**. Quite simply, it was hoped that expenditure on public works such as road building would stimulate the economy and create permanent jobs. However, it was found that many of its employees went back on relief when their contracts ended. In this sense, the scheme offered temporary relief for many of the unemployed but was less successful in stimulating permanent recovery.

## Civilian Conservation Corps

Roosevelt understood that young people needed to gain experience of work. The Civilian Conservation Corps was formed to provide them with useful jobs, for example, in conservation in national parks, forests and public lands. By 1935 it had 500,000 recruits: among its work was the installation of 65,100 miles of telephone lines in inaccessible areas and planting 1.3 billion trees. It gave countless young men a new sense of self-respect and comradeship.

## Identify an argument   a

Below are a series of definitions, a sample exam question and two sample conclusions. One of the conclusions achieves a high mark because it contains an argument. The other achieves a lower mark because it contains only description and assertion. Identify which is which. The mark scheme on page 102 will help you.

- Description: a detailed account.
- Assertion: a statement of fact or an opinion which is not supported by a reason.
- Reason: a statement which explains or justifies something.
- Argument: an assertion justified with a reason.

How far did the First New Deal solve the impact of the Depression?

> The First New Deal set up a series of alphabet agencies to solve the problems caused by the Depression. These included the Agricultural Adjustment Agency, which paid farmers to produce less, and the National Recovery Administration, which aimed to stimulate industrial recovery. FERA produced direct relief for the first time.

> The New Deal was designed in large part to solve the problems caused by the Depression. Significant new legislation was passed during the first hundred days. Emergency relief, for example, through FERA saw direct government involvement, while alphabet agencies were set up to help recovery in both the industrial and agricultural sectors by NIRA (National Industry Recovery Act) and AAA (Agricultural Adjustment Act) respectively. Although FERA's funding was insufficient to solve the impact of the Depression it nevertheless set a precedent in terms of direct relief. One might argue it was the precedents set by the Government in the First New Deal that had a greater impact than the success in solving the problems caused by the Depression. However, the AAA, by paying farmers to produce less, helped stabilise prices and returned some measure of prosperity to those aspects of agriculture it affected.

## Eliminate irrelevance   a

Below are a sample AS Level exam question and a paragraph written in answer to this question. Read the paragraph and identify parts of the paragraph that are not directly relevant to the question. Draw a line through the information that is irrelevant and justify your deletions in the margin.

How successful was the First New Deal in the years 1933–35? AS

> The First New Deal was successful in some ways and less successful in others. It was certainly successful in the level of activity that saw 16 alphabet agencies set up in the first hundred days, which aimed to solve problems caused by the Depression both in terms of recovery and relief. This activity marked a shift in terms of direct action. Furthermore, Roosevelt understood that young people needed to gain experience of work. The Civilian Conservation Corps was formed to provide them with useful jobs, for example, in conservation in national parks, forests and public lands. By 1935 it had 500,000 recruits: among its work was the installation of 65,100 miles of telephone lines in inaccessible areas and planting 1.3 billion trees. It gave countless young men a new sense of self-respect and comradeship. However, the agencies of the First New Deal were only partially successful in their aims. Many states refused to spend the monies allocated by FERA, for example, while the work creation schemes only provided temporary employment.

# Reforming the financial system

With the entire financial system of banking and credit on the verge of collapse, Roosevelt's task was not simply to avert the crisis but reform the nation's finances. The aim was that such a situation could never reoccur.

The banking system faced catastrophe as Roosevelt came to power. By 1932 banks were closing at a rate of 40 per day; by 1933 many states such as Nevada had temporarily closed all their banks while awaiting federal government action.

## The Emergency Banking Relief Act (EBRA)

On 6 March 1933, Roosevelt shut all the banks for four days while he aimed to restore confidence in them.
- He gave the first of his fireside chats, explaining the nature of the banking crisis and how ordinary people could help – by depositing their money with banks once they reopened.
- Meanwhile EBRA was introduced with the primary aim of restoring confidence in the banking system. It gave the Treasury the authority to investigate any banks threatened with collapse and the Reconstruction Finance Corporation was authorised to buy up their debts.

These measures worked. Confidence returned as by 1 April, savers had returned $1 billion to bank deposits.

### The Glass–Steagall Act

In spite of the success of Roosevelt's early financial policies, the Glass–Steagall Act was necessary to reform the banking system to ensure it was safe from future collapse.

This was a longer term measure that regulated banking activity:
- it banned savings banks from speculative investment
- it gave the Federal Reserve Board more supervisory powers over banking activities, such as **open market operations** and selling **government securities**
- it established the Federal Deposit Insurance Corporation, which insured individual bank deposits to the value of $2,500 against bank failures. State banks were forced to join the Federal Reserve system to qualify
- it tried to prevent allegations of malpractice by refusing to allow bank officials to take out personal loans from their own banks.

### Criticisms

Some were disappointed by the Glass–Steagall Act for various reasons:
- some felt the Government should have taken more direct control of the banks
- some felt many banks were being subsidised to stay in business as a reward for their inefficiency
- some felt that it gave too much power to the Federal Reserve, for example, by encouraging state banks to join.

## Regulation of the Stock Exchange

To avoid another collapse, the Stock Exchange was regulated.
- The Truth in Securities Act 1933 required brokers to offer clients truthful information about securities they were selling.
- The Securities Act 1934 set up the Securities Exchange Commission (SEC) to oversee stock market activities and prevent fraudulent activities such as insider dealing.

These measures were successful despite opposition from Wall Street managers who threatened to move the Stock Exchange to Canada. The Commission was headed by Joseph Kennedy, a former stockbroker who was an expert in the workings of the Stock Exchange. The new Commission was very effective. For example, it arrested and imprisoned Richard Witney, one of Wall Street's most famous stockbrokers, in 1938 for embezzlement.

## Spot the inference

High-level answers avoid excessive summarising or paraphrasing the sources. Instead they make inferences from the sources, as well as analysing their value in terms of their context.

Below are a source and a series of statements. Read the source and decide which of the statements:

- makes inferences from the source (I)
- paraphrases the source (P)
- summarise the source (S)
- cannot be justified from the source (X)

Fill in the boxes below with either I, P, S, or X:

- The banking crisis only lasted one week. ☐
- The banking crisis only lasted one week but the emergency involved more than banking. ☐
- The banking crisis was only one aspect of the economic crisis, and so its solution was only one part of the overall answer. ☐

### SOURCE 1

Extract from *On Our Way*, written by F D Roosevelt, in May 1934. Roosevelt was US President at the time. His book explains the meaning of the New Deal.

Strictly speaking the banking crisis lasted only one week. During the second week from the moment the banks day by day reopened their doors and long lines of depositors placed their money back on deposit, the most critical part of the banking emergency was over.

But the full meaning of that word 'emergency' related to far more than banks: it covered the whole economy and therefore the whole structure of the country. It was an emergency that went to the roots of our agriculture, our commerce and our industry; it was an emergency that had existed for a whole generation in its underlying causes and for three and a half years in its visible effects. It could be cured only by a complete reorganization and a measured control of the economic structure. It could not be cured in a week, in a month, or a year. It called for a long series of new laws, new administrative agencies... Most of all it called for redress and understanding on the part of the people. We could not go back to the old order.

## You're the examiner

Below are a sample exam question and a paragraph written in answer to this question. Read the paragraph and the mark scheme provided on page 102. Decide which level you would award the paragraph and write a justification for your choice.

How far did the First New Deal extend the role of government in the economy in the years 1933–35?

The First New Deal significantly extended the role of government in the economy, although to some extent it built on developments begun by Hoover. The big difference was the extent of federal government intervention, including the provision of direct relief through FERA, which gave $500 million to be divided equally among states to provide relief for the unemployed. Roosevelt remained a fiscal conservative, however, believing in a balanced budget and hoped the relief measures, particularly those involving public works schemes, would eventually be self-supporting and help the nation recover from Depression. Nevertheless, the First New Deal clearly broke with precedent, for example, through the regulation and reform of the banking and financial institutions of the USA. Roosevelt recognised that banking provided the basis of the economy and so was prepared to tackle the banking crisis energetically, initially closing the banks for four days and in the longer term through EBRA, which restructured the banking system. Overall, then, the role of government was significantly extended through the goals of relief, recovery and reform during the years 1933–35.

# Opposition to the First New Deal

The New Deal attracted much opposition, from the right because it was too radical and the left because it wasn't radical enough.

## The right

Many of the businessmen who had supported Roosevelt's measures when capitalism seemed threatened with collapse now opposed them when it appeared to be saved. In particular, they resented the high taxes to pay for New Deal Programmes.

### Liberty Leaguers

The Liberty League was formed in April 1934 by conservative Democrats and Republicans to oppose the New Deal. They believed the free market unregulated by government as the best means of ensuring lasting economic recovery. By 1936 it had 125,000 members – although most of these fell away after Roosevelt's 1936 electoral victory. Liberty Leaguers achieved little.

## The left

Roosevelt was afraid that left-wing groups would join together to form a large new political party to oppose him in the 1936 election. The groups themselves were diverse, advocating different programmes.

### End Poverty in California (EPIC)

EPIC was a scheme suggested by novelist Upton Sinclair in which the unemployed would be put to work in state-run co-operatives. They would be paid in a currency that could only be spent in other co-operatives. While the idea proved initially popular, it was impractical. Nevertheless many seriously considered it until other alternatives appeared as listed below.

### 'Share Our Wealth'

'Share Our Wealth' was a scheme designed to end poverty, advocated by popular Louisiana senator, **Huey Long**. Long proposed:

- all private fortunes over $3 million should be confiscated and the money redistributed
- the Government should fund old age pensions and introduce a minimum wage
- every family would be guaranteed an income of $2,000–$3,000 per year, with free college education for suitable candidates.

Roosevelt feared Huey Long would stand against him in the 1936 presidential election. However, Long was assassinated in September 1935. Consequently, 'Share Our Wealth' ceased to be an influential political scheme.

### Old Age Revolving Pensions Inc

Dr Francis Townsend advocated a scheme to solve poverty through pensions. He proposed giving a pension of $200 per month to everyone over the age of 60 on the understanding that they spent it all and saved nothing. He argued that the scheme would:

- boost consumption and thereby demand
- create jobs for young people by forcing all over-60s to retire.

While the idea was impractical, it nevertheless attracted 500,000 members of 'Townsend Clubs'.

### Father Charles Coughlin and the National Society for Social Justice

Coughlin was a Catholic priest with a hugely popular radio show called *The Golden Hour of the Little Flower*. His National Society for Social Justice, formed in 1934, favoured redistribution of wealth. Due to the similarity of their programmes, Coughlin favoured an alliance with Huey Long. However, the possibility of an alliance died with Long himself. From the mid-1930s, Coughlin lost support as he became increasingly **anti-Semitic** and supportive of the European dictators.

Political groups favouring more radical measures were known as Thunder on the Left, advocating policies such as **nationalisation of public utilities** and using empty factories to provide jobs for the unemployed. Leaders included Governor Floyd B Olson of Minnesota until his death in 1936 and the brothers Robert Jnr and Philip Lafayette.

## 1934 Mid-term Congressional Elections

In the **mid-term Congressional Elections** of 1934, the **Democrats** made gains in both houses, with 69 out of 96 seats in the **Senate**. This gave Roosevelt the confidence to prepare a Second New Deal and be less concerned about his opponents both on the left and right.

## 1936 Presidential Election

Roosevelt easily won the 1936 election, carrying all but two states. However, he was to meet his biggest opponents in his second administration in the form of the Supreme Court (see page 46).

## (i) Develop the detail

Below are a sample exam question and a paragraph written in answer to this question. The paragraph contains a limited amount of detail. Annotate the paragraph to add additional detail to the answer.

How accurate is it to say that the opposition from the left seriously threatened both the First New Deal and Roosevelt's presidency?

Many left-wing groups associated with Thunder on the Left opposed Roosevelt's programmes. They felt they were not radical enough. Roosevelt also faced opposition from rivals for the Democratic nomination for presidency in 1935. Others also had alternatives to the New Deal programmes. It seemed that opposition was very comprehensive and a significant threat. However, the majority of the electorate were loyal to Roosevelt during the period of the First New Deal. He was able to dismiss the opposition from the left.

## (i) Turning assertion into argument

Below are a sample exam question and a series of assertions. Read the exam question and then add a justification to each of the assertions to turn it into an argument.

How significant was the left-wing opposition to Roosevelt in threatening his policies of recovery, relief and reform during the First New Deal?

There was a small amount of left-wing opposition to Roosevelt during the First New Deal because...

_____

_____

Roosevelt faced significant left-wing opposition to the First New Deal because...

_____

_____

The left-wing opposition to the First New Deal was only partial and it did not affect any of the measures in the sense that...

_____

_____

The left-wing opposition to the First New Deal was significant enough to threaten both the programmes of relief, recovery and reform and indeed Roosevelt's chances of being selected by the Democratic Party for a second term of office. This was because...

_____

_____

# The Second New Deal, 1935–38

In 1935 Roosevelt introduced a Second New Deal, which was in many ways more radical than the first, particularly in terms of favouring the poorer classes over the rich.

## Reasons for a more radical programme

- Roosevelt needed to respond to the demands of his more radical supporters lest they oppose him.
- Congress itself demanded radical measures and Roosevelt did not want to lose the initiative: he wanted to introduce his own legislation not rubber stamp measures introduced by Congress.
- He was increasingly frustrated by the wealthy classes and big business who opposed him despite the New Deal having saved the system of capitalism.
- He wanted to appeal to the less advantaged ranks in society whom he believed had been forgotten in the past.

## Second New Deal Legislation

### Emergency Relief Appropriation Act 1935

This measure comprised the biggest **appropriation** in US history at that time for relief, with $45.5 billion being earmarked for public works schemes. It set up the Works Progress Administration (WPA), which had employed 20 per cent of the workforce by 1940 on a variety of schemes. Among its large-scale projects were Fort Knox, the repository of US gold reserves, and the Lincoln Tunnel in New York.

### The Revenue Act 1935

This was often known as the 'Soak the Rich' Act. It increased taxes to pay for New Deal reforms, increasing, for example, the maximum tax on incomes of over $50,000 from 50 to 75 per cent. While the increased taxes raised comparatively little as only one per cent of the population earned salaries of over $10,000, it was the principle the detractors objected to.

### Social Security Act 1935

This was the first federal measure of direct welfare given as a right to all those who qualified. It instituted old age pensions and disability pensions, which, although meagre, set a precedent for future development. Unemployment benefit was offered for a limited period of 16 weeks.

The Act was a major break with federal government tradition of not getting involved in welfare. It did, however, have to be self-financing. Recipients of old age pensions had to pay into the system and the amount they received depended on how much they paid. There were also significant omissions, including domestic and agricultural workers who earned too little to contribute.

### Wagner Act (National Labor Relations Act) 1935

For the first time, trade unions were given legal rights, such as that of collective bargaining, and a three-man National Labour Relations Board was set up to ensure fair play between employers and their workforce in disputes. The Wagner Act was initiated in Congress but supported by Roosevelt.

## Labor Unions in the USA

Employers in the USA had a tradition of hostility to trade unions and many had adopted **'Yellow Dog' clauses**, which prevented their employees from joining them. The National Recovery Act outlawed these clauses and set up a Labor Board to facilitate the right of workers to join unions. However, many employers ignored this. Henry Ford even employed strong-arm men to intimidate workers, deterring them from joining a union or becoming involved in disputes.

## Developing an argument

Below are a sample exam question, a list of key points to be made in the essay, and a paragraph from the essay. Read the question, the plan, and the sample paragraph. Rewrite the paragraph in order to develop an argument. Your paragraph should answer the question directly, and set out the evidence that supports your argument. Crucially, it should develop an argument by setting out a general answer to the question and reasons that support this.

How accurate is it to say that the Second New Deal was more radical than the First New Deal?

Key points:
- Roosevelt needed to develop a more radical programme to appease his more radical supporters
- Emergency Relief Appropriation Act 1935
- The Revenue Act 1935
- Social Security Act 1935
- Wagner Act (National Labor Relations Act) 1935

The Second New Deal was more radical than the First. The New Deal had primarily been concerned to solve the problems caused by the Depression and save the capitalist system from collapse, setting up measures such as emergency relief, agencies such as the NRA to stimulate the economy and reform of the financial system through The Emergency Banking Reform Act and regulation of the Stock Exchange. By comparison, the measures of the Second New Deal were more radical and targeted groups previously neglected by government. The Revenue Act 1935 increased taxes to pay for New Deal reforms and in 1935 also social security was introduced for the first time. The Social Security Act introduced old age pensions and disability pensions and unemployment benefit for a limited period of 16 weeks. The Wagner Act gave trade unions legal rights for the first time. A National Labour Relations Board was set up to arbitrate in labour disputes. Overall, the Second New Deal saw federal government become far more involved in people's lives than ever before.

## The flaw in the argument

a

Below are a sample exam question and a paragraph written in answer to this question. The paragraph contains an argument which attempts to answer the question. However, there is an error in the argument. Use your knowledge of this topic to identify the flaw in the argument.

'The Second New Deal was primarily designed to help "the forgotten man".' How far do you agree with this statement?

The measures of the Second New Deal helped 'the forgotten man' — those social groups who had been excluded from previous legislation. Roosevelt believed that federal government should protect the most vulnerable members of society and he was passionate that the Second New Deal would embrace significant social and lasting reform. The main new measure here was the 1935 Social Security Act, which gave old age pensions, sickness benefit and unemployment benefits for the first time. It wasn't so much that the measures were extensive — pensions, for example, were limited and unemployment benefit was only offered to certain groups for a maximum of 16 weeks — but that it set a precedent for future developments. Roosevelt had to appease Congress, which wanted more radical and far ranging reforms for those previously excluded than he would have liked. He had also grown frustrated with the wealthy and business interests who opposed him after the First New Deal had saved the capitalist system.

# Opposition to the Second New Deal

Roosevelt faced significant opposition to the Second New Deal, made worse as problems emerged in his second term of office. His first major battle was with the Supreme Court.

## The Supreme Court

One main task of the Supreme Court is to ensure that legislation is constitutional, or that the framers actually have the powers to make the laws they envisage. As the New Deal developed in the mid-1930s, the Supreme Court increasingly declared legislation unconstitutional. On 'Black Monday', 27 May 1935, the Supreme Court found several pieces of New Deal legislation unconstitutional, including the NIRA, and in January 1936, the AAA.

The Court was also prepared to strike down state measures it considered unconstitutional. In June 1936, for example, it refused to allow a New York state law providing for a minimum wage for women and child workers.

## The 'Sick Chicken' case

In the 'Sick Chicken' case the Supreme Court found that the Federal Government had acted unconstitutionally and as a result NIRA was wound up. A New York firm of butchers, the Schechter Brothers were found to be selling chicken unfit for human consumption, and were prosecuted by the NIRA for contravening the codes of practice they had accepted as signatories to NIRA (see page 38). The Supreme Court upheld their subsequent appeal arguing that the NIRA had no powers to intervene in matters that were the responsibility of the individual states. This made the NIRA codes unconstitutional and meant the NIRA could not survive. When its original remit expired in 1935 it was not renewed.

### The Judiciary Reform Bill

Roosevelt's response was to reform the Supreme Court to make it more amenable. In February 1936 the Judiciary Reform Bill proposed to:
- raise the number of Supreme Court judges from 9 to 15
- retire them compulsorily at 70, to be replaced by presidential appointees.

Roosevelt's aim was to appoint more judges who would support him. However, the Senate saw that this was an attempt to control the Supreme Court and rejected the Bill by 70 votes to 20.

Roosevelt had been defeated, although recognising his huge electoral victory in the 1936 presidential election the Supreme Court did become less obstructive.

## Opposition of the wealthy and conservatives

Roosevelt continued to be opposed by big business and the wealthy. However, Republicans were increasingly joined by more conservative Democrats who thought Roosevelt was becoming too powerful. Indeed, opponents in Congress issued a Conservative Manifesto in December 1937, calling for lower taxes and more restrictions on industrial action.

### Mid-term Congressional Elections 1938

Roosevelt openly supported liberal as opposed to conservative Democrats in the mid-term elections in 1938. This was resented, achieving little except problems in establishing working relations with the new Congress when it met.

## The 'Roosevelt recession', 1937–38

In June 1937, Roosevelt cut expenditure to try to achieve a balanced budget. He hoped that the economy had recovered sufficiently to fill the gaps left by government cutbacks. This was not the case. Unemployment rose from 7,000,000 to 10,390,000 within a year and national income fell by 13 per cent. It seemed it was only government action that had reduced the impact of the Depression and real recovery seemed as far away as ever.

However, the failures of the New Deal were negated by the impact of rearmament as the Second World War broke out elsewhere. Opposition to the New Deal faded as the Deal itself wound down.

**Write the question**

The following sources relate to the conflict between Roosevelt and the Supreme Court. Read the guidance detailing what you need to know about this conflict. Having done this, write an exam-style question using the sources.

How far could the historian make use of Sources 1 and 2 together to investigate…?

_____

_____

Having written the question, you should now plan the answer.

## SOURCE 1

Extract from a fireside chat by President Roosevelt, 9 March 1937.

In the case holding the AAA unconstitutional, Justice [Harlan] Stone said of the majority opinion that it was a 'tortured construction of the Constitution'. And two other justices agreed with him.

In the case holding the New York Minimum Wage Law unconstitutional, Justice Stone said that the majority were actually reading into the Constitution their own 'personal economic predilections', and that if the legislative power is not left free to choose the methods of solving the problems of poverty, subsistence, and health of large numbers in the community, then 'government is to be rendered impotent'. And two other justices agreed with him.

In the face of these dissenting opinions, there is no basis for the claim made by some members of the Court that something in the Constitution has compelled them regretfully to thwart the will of the people. In the face of such dissenting opinions, it is perfectly clear that as Chief Justice Hughes has said, 'We are under a Constitution, but the Constitution is what the judges say it is.'

## SOURCE 2

Extract from _Pure Personal Government: Roosevelt Goes Too Far in Packing the Court,_ written by journalist Dorothy Thompson, published in the _Washington Star,_ 10 February 1937.

This is no proposal to change the Constitution. This is no proposal to limit the powers of the Supreme Court. This is a proposal to capture the Supreme Court. There is a constitutional issue in this country, but it has nothing to do with the age of judges.

If all the justices of the Supreme Court had voted during the last four years with Justice [Louis] Brandeis they could all have been his age, which is 80, and the question of retiring them would not have occurred. Or do you think it would?

If, of the six men over 70, four had been 'liberals' and two 'conservatives', instead of the other way around, do you think that this program would have been proposed?

The theory that if 9 men take 90 days to make up their individual minds, 15 men will take fewer days to make up theirs is cabalistic arithmetic. Nine men of 60 can work faster than 9 men of 70, but 15 men, of whom 6 are over 70, can expedite business in the same time as 9, all of whom are under 70. Apparently that is the logic.

 **Recommended reading**

- Anthony J Badger, _The New Deal: The Depression Years 1933–1940_, (1989)
- Michael E Parrish, _Anxious Decades_, Part Two (1992)
- Amity Shaels, _The Forgotten Man_, Introduction, Chapters 6, 7, 8, 11 and 13 (2009)

# Exam focus

Below is a sample A Level essay question and model answer. Read the answer and the comments around it.

How significant was the opposition to the First and Second New Deals during the period 1933 to 1938 in enabling Roosevelt to pass and implement New Deal programmes?

The New Deal attracted significant opposition, both from different ends of the political spectrum but also from those who feared it was too great an assumption of federal government power. Right-wing groups attacked the First and Second New Deal programmes because they were perceived to be too radical, while the left opposed them because they weren't radical enough. Roosevelt's most difficult battle, however, may have been with the Supreme Court, which increasingly questioned the legality of New Deal measures in the face of the limitations on federal government activity contained within the Constitution, a battle which led in 1937 to an unsuccessful attempt at its reform.

Roosevelt faced an ongoing battle with the interests of big business and the wealthy. Many of the businessmen, for example, who had supported Roosevelt's measures when capitalism seemed threatened with collapse, now opposed them when it appeared to be saved. In particular, they resented the high taxes to pay for New Deal Programmes. Indeed, on April 1934 many wealthy groups formed the Liberty Leaguers to promote private property and private enterprise unregulated by law. However, while these groups irritated Roosevelt, they couldn't significantly harm him. The New Deal had been created to save capitalism both through stimulation of industry through, for example, the National Industry Recovery Act and reform measures, such as the Truth in Securities Act, and wealthy groups couldn't risk the uncertainty and instability of destroying it.

Roosevelt was rather more concerned about opposition from the other side of the political spectrum because this could erode his natural supporters and force him to implement more radical measures than he had wished. Here he faced more radical Democrats who felt his New Deals didn't go far enough, and those who offered alternative programmes. In the case of Huey Long with his 'Share Our Wealth' programme, the idea was far more radical than anything in the First New Deal.

Roosevelt continued to be opposed by big business and the wealthy. However, Republicans were increasingly joined by more conservative Democrats who thought Roosevelt was becoming too powerful. Indeed, opponents in Congress issued a Conservative Manifesto in December 1937 calling for lower taxes and more restrictions on industrial action, which had proliferated following the Wagner Act. This was reflected in the 1938 mid-term Congressional elections, which saw a more conservative Congress concerned that the New Deal was overreaching government authority and Roosevelt was becoming too like a dictator. Clearly the level of opposition from his erstwhile Democratic supporters in alliance with Republican opponents was becoming significant enough to stifle further New Deal measures. Indeed, the programme seemed to be diminishing as the responses to war in Europe began to dominate government activity.

Nevertheless, while opposition from the left and right continued during Roosevelt's more troubled second term, his biggest opposition had come from the Supreme Court. As the First New Deal developed, the Supreme Court increasingly declared legislation unconstitutional. On 'Black Monday', 27 May 1935 the Supreme Court found several pieces of New Deal legislation unconstitutional, including the NIRA. This was a result of the 'Sick Chicken' case in which a firm of New York butchers were prosecuted under NIRA codes for selling chickens unfit for human consumption. A subsequent appeal to the Supreme Court resulted in the

**Focus on question from outset.**

**Introduction sets out question parameters, showing its full range is understood.**

**Assertion supported by evidence to create valid argument.**

**Valid judgement with reasons in support.**

**This paragraph introduces the theme of Roosevelt overreaching his power and acts as a bridge between the political opposition and the constitutional opposition.**

Quick quizzes at **www.hoddereducation.co.uk/myrevisionnotes**

judgement that the case should have been dealt with by New York State and the NIRA had no powers to intervene in state matters. This made the whole concept of NIRA codes of practice unconstitutional and meant the NIRA could not survive. Similarly, the Supreme Court rendered the AAA unconstitutional in January 1936. Therefore, it posed the most serious opposition in enabling Roosevelt to carry out his New Deal policies.

Roosevelt's response to what he felt was prolonged opposition from the Supreme Court was to reform it to make it more amenable. In February 1936 he presented the Judiciary Reform Bill to Congress, which proposed to raise the number of Supreme Court judges from 9 to 15 and to make them retire them at 70. The theory was that Roosevelt could appoint more judges who would support him and get rid of older ones who were more conservative. In fact, his reasoning was faulty – the most liberal judge was in fact the eldest. Moreover, the Senate saw that this was an attempt to control the Supreme Court and rejected the Bill by 70 votes to 20. In taking on the Supreme Court, Roosevelt was seen to have over-reached himself. The Court opposition was significant in that Roosevelt was seen to have lost the battle – even though the Court was more accommodating in future.

Roosevelt managed to contain opposition, which was significant to varying degrees at different times during the period of the First and Second New Deals. Nevertheless, overall it was significant, fuelled in part by the failures of the New Deals. The most significant criticism in reducing the impact of the New Deals was the argument that they were too ambitious for the power of federal government as stated in the constitution. The Supreme Court was bound to take this line as the prime interpreter of the constitution. Moreover, it was a much-respected institution, which was trusted to prevent the development of over-powerful government, and in trying to reform it Roosevelt came across as a dictator. However, one should balance this with the idea that in 1933 most groups in society demanded action to save capitalism and combat the Depression. Roosevelt argued that big business only turned against him when he had achieved what they required, and the New Deals were more conservative than the programmes more radical groups advocated. He once said that everyone was against him but the electorate. How far the electorate would have turned against him but for the very different circumstances of responses to and preparation for war is impossible to say.

**Strikes the balance between the impact of the case and the need to explain what it was about – avoids unnecessary description.**

**Although the issue is crucial to the question set, the focus in this paragraph is on Roosevelt more than the New Deals, although it is difficult to see how this could be avoided in this case. It wouldn't penalise the candidate.**

**Balanced judgements in the conclusion.**

This is a confident, well-structured response whose occasional lapses wouldn't seriously reduce the mark. There is sufficient analysis of key features with valid supporting knowledge to warrant Level 5. The overall judgement is based on relevant criteria. The structure is excellent, with a series of clear arguments precisely communicated.

### Reverse engineering

Read the essay and the comments and try to work out the general points of the plan used to write the essay. Once you have done this, note down the specific examples used to support each general point.

## AS Level question

How successful was the First New Deal in addressing the economic problems caused by the Depression?

## The New Deal and the economy

REVISED

Many have argued that the New Deal failed to achieve its aim of stimulating the economy. The national total of personal income was $86 billion in 1929 falling to $73 billion ten years later. Average wages had fallen from $25.03 per week in 1929 to $23.86 in 1939.

Many agree that the real reason for economic recovery was the demand for munitions and **war materiel** as a result of the amendment of the 1935 Neutrality Acts in November 1939. This meant **belligerents** could buy from the USA – within a year there were orders for 10,800 aircraft.

### The impact of New Deal policies on unemployment

Unemployment halved from around 18 million to around 9 million between 1933 and 1939. This was, however, still a massive figure and most workers left the alphabet agencies at the termination of their contracts to return to joblessness. The Roosevelt recession of 1937 (see page 46) in particular brought home how dependent people were on government schemes – cutbacks led to an increased unemployment figure of 19 per cent.

Table 2.1

| US Unemployment Statistics 1929–41 | | | |
| --- | --- | --- | --- |
| Year | Population | Unemployed | Percentage of labour force |
| 1929 | 88,010,000 | 1,550,000 | 3.14 |
| 1930 | 89,550,000 | 4,340,000 | 8.67 |
| 1931 | 90,710,000 | 8,020,000 | 15.82 |
| 1932 | 91,810,000 | 12,060,000 | 23.53 |
| 1933 | 92,950,000 | 12,830,000 | 24.75 |
| 1934 | 94,190,000 | 11,340,000 | 21.60 |
| 1935 | 95,460,000 | 10,610,000 | 19.97 |
| 1936 | 96,700,000 | 9,030,000 | 16.80 |
| 1937 | 97,870,000 | 7,700,000 | 14.18 |

| US Unemployment Statistics 1929–41 | | | |
| --- | --- | --- | --- |
| Year | Population | Unemployed | Percentage of labour force |
| 1938 | 99,120,000 | 10,390,000 | 18.91 |
| 1939 | 100,360,000 | 9,480,000 | 17.05 |
| 1940 | 101,560,000 | 8,120,000 | 14.45 |
| 1941 | 102,700,000 | 5,560,000 | 9.66 |

### The impact of the alphabet agencies

The alphabet agencies such as the PWA and WPA had been created as pump-primers to stimulate the economy. The theory was that public works schemes would not only create jobs through the actual ventures themselves but also stimulate recovery by orders for materials and equipment, and providing employment to maintain the schemes.

### Numbers

Undoubtedly, alphabet agencies provided many with temporary jobs: at its peak in July 1934, the PWA employed 643,299. However, by January 1938, as a result of the cutbacks that led to the recession, this figure had fallen to 98,743, before rising again to 342,202 in June 1939. It wasn't until the wartime economy began to develop that numbers significantly fell, from 76,042 in September 1940 to 9,507 when it was wound up in June 1941.

### Development of the Roosevelt recession

Roosevelt's advisers had warned him on several occasions that federal spending should not be reduced until private enterprise had expanded enough to be in a position to recruit at high levels. However, Roosevelt was more concerned to achieve a balanced budget, and in 1937 agreed to cutbacks of $66 million. The result was the Roosevelt recession. By 1938 unemployment rose to over 10 million before falling again a year later.

# Select the detail

Below is a sample A Level exam question with the accompanying sources. Having read the question and the sources, complete the following activity.

How far could the historian make use of Sources 1 and 2 together to investigate the impact of the New Deal on the economy between 1933 and 1938?

Below are three claims that you could make when answering the question. Read the claims and then select quotes from the sources to support them. Keep the quotes short; never copy more than a sentence.

1 The New Deal helped prepare the economy for war...

2 The New Deal lost momentum as economic priorities changed...

3 Source 2 is valuable to a historian because it gives the view of a senior member in Roosevelt's government because...

## SOURCE 1

From *Roosevelt in Retrospect: A Profile in History,* by John Gunter, published in 1950. Gunter was an authoritative and well respected US journalist.

Of course the New Deal helped considerably to make the American war effort possible. The miracles of production the factories of the New Deal performed with only a minimum of labor trouble would not have been so easily achieved except for the groundwork FDR laid in the years of peace. Emotionally too the people had been prepared for this stupendous crisis by the positiveness of the educational impact and the reformist energy of the New Deal.

As war came closer, FDR had to let more things go in the domestic sphere and the New Deal inevitably dwindled off. If the USA was going to fight a war every ounce of the nation's productive effort must be mobilised. To get production going in a really big way, FDR had to conciliate big businessmen, industrial leaders and the Detroit and Pennsylvania tycoons: the New Deal correspondingly lost prestige and influence. He had to have industry and he had to ensure it a handsome profit.

## SOURCE 2

From *The Roosevelt I Knew,* by Frances Perkins (1948). Perkins served as Roosevelt's Secretary of Labor from 1933 to 1945.

Roosevelt moved fast to demonstrate that something could be done. He took action that was needed, but more than that, he explained over the radio what that action was, how it was going to be taken, what he hoped it would do and what the people's role would be.

He did not think we had discovered any panaceas. He knew these were temporary emergency measures. He once said at a cabinet meeting about a proposal for further expenditure for public works or the WPA, 'We have to do it. It is like putting all you've got into stopping up the hole in the dyke. You have to keep that hole from getting any larger. We must do what we can at this time. We haven't any more time.'

... The speedy enactment of the programme that came to be known as the New Deal revived the faith of the people. It put us back in the upgrade. It gave us knowledge of industrial processes and complications which had never been in the possession of the government before. It constituted an education for the American people and for their government.

## National infrastructure

The New Deal transformed the **national infrastructure** of the USA in terms of public works programmes, which created new roads, public buildings and facilities, and developments in rural areas such as forestation and windbreaks. Most of these were created by alphabet agencies such as the PWA, but many were also the result of existing government organisations such as the Bureau of Public Roads in the Department of Agriculture. Between 1933 and 1939, indeed, the Government financed $16 billion grants and payments and $10 billion in loans for public works. At any time, public works schemes could account for 66 per cent of emergency funds.

## Public works by alphabet agencies

Many alphabet agencies were responsible for public works and their work tended to overlap. The WPA were supposedly responsible for smaller-scale projects such as schools, and the WPA for large-scale enterprises such as dams and bridges, but in reality both built streets, highways, dams and tunnels. Indeed, 80 per cent of new sewers and 50 per cent of waterworks were built by one or the other.

The PWA in fact funded 35,000 projects and WPA 300,000. Among the latter were one and a half million miles of roads.

## Public works in rural areas

Public works in rural areas included picnic trails and conservation work by the Civilian Conservation Corps (CCC) and the provision of electricity by the Rural Electrification Administration (REA), formed in May 1935. As a result of its work, the numbers of farmers with access to electricity rose from 12.6 per cent in 1936 to 35 per cent by 1941: 773 systems with 348,000 miles of transmission lines had been laid in six years.

## Tennessee Valley Authority (TVA)

The Tennessee Valley Authority, formed in May 1933 was created to harness the power of the river Tennessee, which ran through seven relatively poor states. The intention was to generate electricity in an area where only two per cent of farms had access to it. More importantly, however, through a central planning authority it encouraged people to work together for the benefit of the entire region. More specifically, the TVA had various tasks:

- to construct 20 dams to control flooding and harness the power of the river and generate hydro-electric power
- to develop ecological schemes such as tree planting to prevent the major problem of soil erosion and encourage farming education, such as the development of contour ploughing
- to provide welfare and educational programmes
- to provide jobs by setting up fertiliser manure factories, for example.

Overall, public works schemes had a major impact on the national infrastructure, providing buildings and facilities where none previously existed. The director of the PWA, Harold Ickes, asserted that Roosevelt's government had a greater impact on the physical environment than any previous one. His colleague at the WPA, Harry Hopkins, argued that the projects built by his agency had advanced the standard of living by 50 years.

## Identify the concept

Below are five sample exam questions based on some of the following concepts:

- cause – questions concern the reasons for something, or why something happened
- consequence – questions concern the impact of an event, an action or a policy
- change/continuity – questions ask you to investigate the extent to which things changed or stayed the same
- similarity/difference – questions ask you to investigate the extent to which two events, actions or policies were similar
- significance – questions concern the importance of an event, an action or a policy.

Read each of the questions and work out which of the concepts they are based on.

1  'The New Deal transformed the national infrastructure of the USA.' How far do you agree with this statement?

2  The New Deal was radically different from US economic policy under Calvin Coolidge.' How far do you agree with this statement?

3  To what extent did the New Deal solve the problems caused by the Depression?

4  How accurate is it to say that the battle with the Supreme Court was the most important opposition faced by Roosevelt during the 1930s?

5  The New Deal merely continued Hoover's approach to solving America's economic problems.' How far do you agree with this statement?

## Develop the detail

Below are a sample exam question and a paragraph written in answer to this question. The paragraph contains a limited amount of detail. Annotate the paragraph to add additional detail to the answer.

'The New Deal transformed the national infrastructure of the USA.' How far do you agree with this statement?

The New Deal transformed the national infrastructure of the USA. Roosevelt set up alphabet agencies to undertake public works. In addition, some government organisations already existed. Large amounts of funding were made available for the construction of public works. The PWA broadly undertook larger-scale projects and WPA smaller ones. Alphabet agencies such as the CCC also did public works in rural areas. The REA brought electricity to rural areas. The TVA was set up to work over a region of seven states, encouraging the inhabitants to co-operate together. Altogether Roosevelt's government had a dramatic impact on the physical landscape and infrastructure of the USA.

# The impact of the New Deal on women: the economy in 1940

The New Deal helped raise the profile of many successful women but its impact on women as a whole was limited.

## Effects of New Deal legislation on women

- The 1933 Economy Act: this Act was designed in part to save government spending on salaries. It forbade members of the same family from working for the Federal Government 75 per cent of those who lost their jobs through this were women.
- NRA codes allowed for unequal pay.
- Some alphabet agencies such as the CCC banned women entirely.

## The New Deal years

The New Deal years saw no discernible improvements in the status of women. They still faced a greater risk of unemployment than men, particularly if they were married, and the professions remained still male dominated.

Labour unions did not encourage women in the workplace; their main stance was that men were the principle wage-earners and large numbers of women employees would depress wages. On average, during the 1930s the average yearly salary for women, at $525, was half that of men.

## Women in government

The New Deal years saw more women in important government roles. Eleanor Roosevelt was a hugely influential, high-profile First Lady, while Ruth Bryan Owen became the first female Ambassador (to Denmark) in 1933. Frances Perkins worked as Secretary for Labor throughout Roosevelt's terms of office and helped draw up the 1935 Social Security Act.

## Eleanor Roosevelt

First Lady **Eleanor Roosevelt** acted as a significant role-model for women both during the period of her husband's administration and after. She took a far more proactive role than any previous First Lady, becoming involved particularly in the role and status of women and social issues. As a journalist, her features in *Women's Home Journal* regularly attracted thousands of responses, while her column 'My Day' was **syndicated** to 62 newspapers.

She also acted as her husband's eyes and ears, visiting the country to inspect New Deal and wartime programmes. Indeed, as an active civil rights campaigner she may have been instrumental in ensuring black Americans were given combat roles in the US air force.

## The state of the US economy in 1940

The year 1940 was one of economic transformation – GDP rose by 10 per cent to $100 billion from the previous year. Exports reached $4.02 billion. The USA was swamped with orders for war materiel, and factories were refocusing to produce these.

### Reuther's plan, 1940

It was a big decision for manufacturers to convert their factories to war production. Walter Reuther, a key official in the United Auto Workers labour union developed his plan to convert automobile plants into centres of aircraft production. This alerted the public to the slow progress currently being made and helped the process develop more swiftly.

Table 2.2: Statistics recording the differences between the economy in 1933 and 1940

| Measurement | 1933 | 1940 |
|---|---|---|
| GNP | $68.3 billion | $113 billion |
| Index of industrial production | 69 | 126 |
| Unemployment | 25.2% | 13.9% |

On the basis of these figures, the economy appeared twice as healthy in 1940 as it had been in 1933. It is impossible to say how the economy would have fared had the Second World War not broken out, but there is little doubt that this, rather than the New Deal, was the real catalyst for recovery.

**Write the question**

The following sources relate to the role and status of women during the Depression and New Deal years. Read the guidance detailing what you need to know about women during this period. Having done this, write an exam-style question using the sources.

How far could the historian make use of Sources 1 and 2 together to investigate...?

_____

_____

Explain your answer, using both sources, the information given about them and your own knowledge of the historical context.

How much weight do you give the evidence of Source 2 for an enquiry into...?

_____

_____

Explain your answer using the source, the information given about it and your own knowledge of the historical content. **AS**

## SOURCE 1

From *The Lasting Values of the WPA*, by Ellen S. Woodward, from WPA papers in US National Archives. Woodward is justifying the WPA in terms of provision of work for women.

If your community has no bricklayers or carpenters in need of employment, obviously a construction project requiring much skilled brickwork or carpentry would fail to meet the requirement.

In planning a project to supply jobs for unemployed women, by the same token, the yardstick would scarcely be the needs of the highway or sewerage departments. Widows, school teachers, nurses, and dieticians cannot be put to work digging ditches.

Yet, when some destitute widows whose only training had been in the daily routine of household tasks, were given jobs as 'housekeepers' assistants', and were sent to the homes of poor people in one of our large Metropolitan cities, to assist with the housework during a mother's illness or absence, loud were the jeers and cries of 'boondoggling' [wasting public money].

Ignoring the primary object of this particular project – to give work to women who sorely needed it – and distorting the secondary aim, to give them something useful to do within their own community; the editors of hostile newspapers branded 'housekeepers' assistants' as 'government meddlers in the proper business of the mothers of the land.'

## SOURCE 2

From Eleanor Roosevelt, 'What Ten Million Women Want', published in *The Home* magazine, March 1932. Eleanor Roosevelt was married to the future president Franklin D Roosevelt and was known for her feminist views.

... every woman who succeeds creates confidence.

Judge Florence Allen on the Supreme Court Bench in Ohio, Frances Perkins as Labor Commissioner in New York, have done much to make women feel that a really fine woman, well trained in her work, can give as good an account of her stewardship as any man, and eventually women, and perhaps even men, may come to feel that sex should not enter into the question of fitness for office.

When it comes to the matter of having a woman as a member of the President's Cabinet, there are I think, many women who feel that the time has come to recognize the fact that women have practically just as many votes as men and deserve at least a certain amount of recognition.

Take the Department of Labor for instance. Why should not the Secretary of Labor be a woman, and would not a woman's point of view be valuable in the President's Council? There are many other places to which women may aspire, and the time will come when there will be new departments, some of which will undoubtedly need women at their heads.

## The New Deal and black Americans

Many black Americans benefited from New Deal policies but its overall impact on them was limited. Whatever his personal views, Roosevelt needed the votes of Southern Democrats who were often deeply racist. He did nothing, for example, to support anti-lynching bills, which were introduced and defeated in Congress in the years 1934 and 1937.

Not only was there no civil rights legislation but many New Deal measures worked against black Americans. Moreover, the New Deal did little to stop discrimination and injustice.

Nevertheless, many black Americans felt the government was at least listening to them for the first time – that they had a voice. This was possibly why so many supported Roosevelt and the New Deal.

## Changing voting behaviour

One of the most important political developments was the shift in voting behaviour among blacks who were able to vote. Traditionally, they voted Republican because this was the party that had ended slavery. In the 1932 presidential election, Roosevelt won only four of fifteen all-black **wards** in nine US cities: in 1936 this figure had risen to nine and in 1940 all fifteen. In the Harlem district of New York, Roosevelt won 85 per cent of the vote in the 1936 election.

### Reasons for this shift

The reasons for the shift were fundamentally a belief that the New Deal was making things better for black Americans – even though often it was not. This was the result not only of measures such as the 1935 Social Security Act which benefited blacks on equal terms as whites, but also the higher profile that black Americans seemed to have both in government and with influential leaders.

- Many New Deal administrators were sympathetic towards black Americans and encouraged them to join programmes such as the PWA.
- Eleanor Roosevelt (see page 54) vigorously opposed racism and encouraged black American leaders to meet with Roosevelt.
- During the New Deal years, three times more black Americans found employment in government, for example, Mary McLeod Bethune at the National Youth Administration. Indeed, the NYA applied positive discrimination to employ more black Americans than any other agency, and helped 300,000 young black Americans through its work.

## Alphabet agencies and black Americans

Many alphabet agencies employed black Americans although they could face discrimination, notably in the CCC where many leaders came from the South. Black American recruitment here moreover rose from only three per cent of its workforce in 1933 to 11 per cent by 1938. The PWA on the other hand introduced a quota system for minimum levels of black employment for all construction projects. As many as 15 per cent of the WPA workforce at any one time were black Americans.

Nevertheless, some New Deal measures worked against black Americans.

### NRA

Most NRA codes of practice allowed for unequal pay between blacks and whites. Many blacks called it the 'Negro Run Around' because it was so blatantly unfair.

### Agricultural Adjustment Act

Many black Americans were sharecroppers who paid a percentage of their produce as rent. Landowners, however, were paid to produce less by the AAA, so did not require the produce. Many sharecroppers were therefore thrown off the land as they could no longer make a living through farming.

**Select the detail**

Below is a sample A Level exam question with the accompanying sources. Having read the question and the sources, complete the following activity.

How far could the historian make use of Sources 1 and 2 together to investigate the problems faced by black Americans working in alphabet agencies during the New Deal years?

Below are three claims that you could make when answering the question. Read the claims and then select quotes from the sources to support them. Remember to keep the quotes short; never copy more than a sentence. Sometimes a few words embedded in a sentence is all you need to support your claims.

1 The CCC practised racial discrimination

2 Not all officers in the CCC were racist

3 Source 1 is useful to the historian because it offers an example of racism ...

## SOURCE 1

From CCC, 'Youth Refuses To Fan Flies Off Officer; Is Fired', taken from the newspaper *Norfolk Journal and Guide*, 13 January 1934.

NEW YORK, N.Y. – It required just one month and six days to get an honorable discharge from the Civilian Conservation Corps and his last month's pay for Eddie Simons, Harlem youth, after the N.A.A.C.P. took up his case. The story is an interesting one, illustrating as it does some of the difficulties confronting young Negroes in the forestry service officered largely by white Southerners, as well as the willingness of the administration to do justice when pressed for action.

Young Simons was dishonorably discharged and his last month's pay withheld at Camp No. 5, North Lisbon, N.J., on September 26, when he refused to stand and fan flies from a white officer, Lt. J. A. Elmore of the 16th Infantry, temporarily in charge of the camp.

Simons told the officer he did not think fanning flies was part of his duty. Lt. Elmore thereupon dishonorably discharged the lad and denied him his last month's pay although admitting that Simons' record was good.

[Simons was awarded an honourable discharge and received his back pay.]

## SOURCE 2

From *A Negro in the CCC*, by Luther C. Wandall, published in the magazine *Crisis* in August 1935. The author was a black American discussing his first days in the CCC.

1 We reached Camp Dix about 7:30 that evening. As we rolled up in front of headquarters an officer came out to the bus and told us: "You will double-time as you leave this bus, remove your hat when you hit the door, and when you are asked questions, answer 'Yes, sir,' and 'No, sir.'" ...

3 But before we left the bus the officer shouted emphatically: "Colored boys fall out in the rear." The colored from several buses were herded together, and stood in line until after the white boys had been registered and taken to their tents. This seemed to be the established order of procedure at Camp Dix.

4 This separation of the colored from the whites was completely and rigidly maintained at this camp. One Puerto Rican, who was darker than I, and who preferred to be with the colored, was regarded as pitifully uninformed by the officers.

5 While we stood in line there, as well as afterwards, I was interested to observe these officers. They were contradictory, and by no means simple or uniform in type. Many of them were southerners, how many I could not tell. Out of their official character they were usually courteous, kindly, refined, and even intimate. They offered extra money to any of us who could sing or dance. On the other hand, some were vicious and ill-tempered, and apparently restrained only by fear.

# The impact of the war on black Americans

The war had a huge impact on black Americans. They found plentiful employment during the war years and served enthusiastically in the military, albeit in **segregated units**.

## Contribution to the war effort

### Service in the military

Such was the level of discrimination that in 1941 there were only 4,000 black Americans in the military and only 12 officers. Many enlistees were turned down by all-white recruitments boards. This situation only improved when:

● Roosevelt pledged black Americans would be recruited according to their percentage within the population
● the Selective Training Act was passed in 1941 which outlawed discrimination during training.

While both of these measures were negated, there were nevertheless 1.2 million black Americans serving in the armed forces by 1945.

### Employment within the USA

The vast employment opportunities saw millions of black Americans working in wartime production. Indeed, over 300,000 black American women found employment in war-related industries because the demand for labour was so acute. All faced discrimination although conditions did generally improve if only because they had regular income. Nevertheless, the widespread employment of blacks involving the migration of over 5 million to urban areas caused considerable unrest throughout the USA and led to serious rioting in various locations.

### The race riots of 1943

There were severe riots in 1943, particularly over issues such as the shortage of housing, which was strictly segregated. Riots in Detroit in June 1943 led to the deaths of 34 people, 25 of them black. The bone of contention here was whether a new housing development should be exclusively for blacks or whites.

In two days of rioting in Harlem in August 1943 six were killed and 1,485 stores broken into and looted: the overall cost of damage was estimated at between $250,000 and $500,000.

### The Double V campaign

The Double V campaign was initiated in the black press focusing on victory both over the Axis powers abroad and discrimination at home. The campaign featured patriotic articles, promotion of the sale of **war bonds** and endorsements by white celebrities. The message, however, was that civil rights in the US were long overdue.

## The impact of the Fair Employment Practices Commission

Owing to the prejudice they continued to face, black Americans threatened a March on Washington in 1941 to protest unfair treatment. Roosevelt was worried by this: Nazis could rightly accuse the USA of hypocrisy in condemning their treatment of Jews while denying black Americans civil rights. However, while he could do little in private concerns, he could fight unfair treatment in government operations. Executive Order 8802 persuaded organisers to call off the proposed march.

### Government action to prevent discrimination

The Fair Employment Practices Commission was set up in 1941 to enforce Executive Order 8802, which outlawed discrimination in the defence industry. As a result of its work the black American workforce in defence plants rose by four per cent. Its role expanded to include discrimination against any groups, for example, women and its budget rose to $500,000.

### War Labor Board

The War Labor Board was set up in 1942 to prevent industrial disputes which might impede the war effort and protect the rights of workers in war industries. One of its key policies was equal pay for equal work irrespective of race or gender.

## ⏣ RAG – rate the source

In Section A of the exam you will be asked to analyse two sources. You will need to weigh up the evidence of the sources. One way of doing this is to distinguish between the evidence, the opinions and the arguments contained in the sources.

Below are two sample sources, and a sample Section A question. Study the extracts and, using three coloured pens, underline the text in Red, Amber or Green to show:

- Red: arguments presented by the source
- Amber: opinions offered by the sources
- Green: the evidence the source contains.

In the margins, justify why you have highlighted the source, with reference to the historical context of the time.

> How far could the historian make use of Sources 1 and 2 together to investigate how far black Americans participated in the war effort on the Home Front during the Second World War?

### SOURCE 1

Equal pay for black American workers: The 1943 War Labor Board decision that black American workers should receive equal pay.

... the National War Labor Board abolishes the classifications 'colored laborer' and 'white laborer' and reclassifies both simply as 'laborers' with the same rates of pay for all in that classification without discrimination on account of color. The Negro workers in this classification are hereby granted wage increases which place them on a basis of economic parity with the white workers in the same classification... This equalization of economic opportunity is not a violation of the sound American provision of differentials in pay for differences in skills. It is rather a bit of realization of the no less sound American principle of equal pay for equal work as one of those equal rights in the promise of American democracy regardless of color, race, sex, religion, or national origin.

... Economic and political discrimination on account of race or creed is in line with the Nazi program. ... The American answer to differences in color and creed is not a concentration camp but cooperation. The answer to human error is not terror but light and liberty under the moral law. By this light and liberty, the Negro has made a contribution in work and faith, song and story, laughter and struggle which are an enduring part of the spiritual heritage of America.

There is no more loyal group of our fellow citizens than the American Negroes, north and south...

### SOURCE 2

*The Pittsburgh Courier,* 14 February 1942, "The Courier's Double 'V' For a Double Victory Campaign Gets Country-Wide Support."

Last week, without any public announcement or fanfare, the editors of *The Courier* introduced its war slogan – a double 'V' for a double victory to colored America. We did this advisedly because we wanted to test the response and popularity of such a slogan with our readers. The response has been overwhelming. Our office has been inundated with hundreds of telegrams and letters of congratulations proving that without any explanation, this slogan represents the true battle cry of colored America. This week we gratefully acknowledge this voluntary response and offer the following explanation: Americans all, are involved in a gigantic war effort to assure the victory for the cause of freedom – the four freedoms that have been so nobly expressed by President Roosevelt and Prime Minister Churchill. We, as colored Americans, are determined to protect our country, our form of government and the freedoms which we cherish for ourselves and the rest of the world, therefore we have adopted the Double 'V' war cry – victory over our enemies on the battlefields abroad. Thus in our fight for freedom we wage a two-pronged attack against our enslavers at home and those abroad who would enslave us.

## Native Americans

Native Americans were among the poorest of US inhabitants. Many eked out a living on **reservations**. However, the Roosevelt's administration targeted Native Americans to improve their standards of living, and a sympathetic Commissioner for the **Bureau of Indian Affairs**, John Collier, was determined to adopt a system of self-government based on their traditional beliefs and values.

## Assimilation and Allotment

The existing policy towards Native Americans was based on **Assimilation** and **Allotment**. The policy of Assimilation expected Native Americans to live as white US citizens in family units, absorbing mainstream culture. Allotment saw communal land sold off into individual family holdings of 160 acres. However, by 1933, much of the land had been sold to whites or large corporations, which exploited it for raw materials.

In 1926 a Department of Interior Enquiry found that the impact of these policies on Native Americans had been a disaster as a result of these land losses and Allotment in particular should be reversed. However, nothing was done until Roosevelt's administration.

## Indian Reorganization Act 1934 (also known as the Wheeler-Howard Act)

The Indian Reorganization Act of 1934 gave autonomy to Native Americans in the sense of self-government. The Act recognised their own customs and legal systems:

● Each **reservation** could govern itself and have its own legal system and police
● New **tribal corporations** were set up to manage tribal resources collectively and control land sales.

The intention was to maintain the reservations' land holdings and allow them to be governed according to Native American values and traditions.

## Criticisms

Critics, however, argued that respect for tribal culture disadvantaged Native Americans who needed in fact to reduce their dependence on tribal customs and embrace mainstream US culture if they were to thrive in it. They referred to being forced '**back to the blanket**'.

Indeed, when asked to ratify the Act, 75 out of 245 tribes voted against it. The Act marked a division between those Native Americans who valued their customs and traditions and were content to live on reservations and those who sought to join the mainstream USA.

## The New Deal and Native Americans

The New Deal did little for Native Americans economically.

● Collier seemed indifferent to the efforts of large corporations to exploit natural resources on reservation land.
● There were no specific measures aimed at relief for Native Americans. Officials did encourage them to join agencies, such as the CCC and PWA, but the level of overall poverty was so great that they could only have a very limited impact.
● In 1939 the average annual income among Native Americans living on reservations was $500 as compared with a national average of $2,300. Meanwhile, 25 per cent of reservation Native Americans had no formal education.

In 1943 a Senate enquiry found widespread poverty on the reservations persisted despite the boost of a wartime economy.

## Native Americans in the war

The war had a significant impact on Native Americans who joined the armed forces and found work in wartime production.

At any time during the war it was estimated there were 25,000 Native Americans in fighting units. In the Pacific, they were employed to transmit messages in their own languages as the Japanese had no way of translating them. Many Native Americans left the reservations to work in war production or in large-scale agriculture. Mixing with mainstream society led many to further question the validity of the 1934 Indian Reorganization Act and tribal organisation. Increasingly, many felt they should leave the reservations and join mainstream US society. Many Native Americans believed that remaining on the reservations was a recipe for continued poverty. This argument was to resonate throughout the period covered by this book and beyond.

## Explain the difference

The following sources give different attitudes to the Indian Reorganization Act of 1934 (also known as the Wheeler-Howard Act). List the ways in which the sources differ. Explain the differences between the sources using the provenance of the sources, and the historical context. The provenance appears at the top of the source. Make sure you stay focused on the differences that are relevant to the A Level question below.

> How far could the historian make use of Sources 1 and 2 together to investigate differing attitudes to the Indian Reorganization Act of 1934?
>
> Explain your answer, using both sources, the information given about them and your own knowledge of the historical context.

### SOURCE 1

'We Have Got a Good Friend in John Collier': A Taos Pueblo Tries to Sell the Indian New Deal.

Antonio Luhan was a Taos Pueblo Native American. This undated letter to John Collier about the Indian Reorganization Act appears in a book written by his wife in 1935.

... I explained... what the Bill meant, and all about Self-Government. I told them how the Rio Grande Indians rule by self-government, by having a Governor and a Lieutenant-governor and the twelve officers. And the War Chief has a Lieutenant and he has twelve members for himself. I explained what the War Chief has to do.

The War Chief has to take care of and look after all the land outside, look after the boundaries and their fences, and the Governor takes care of everything inside the village, family troubles and the way the people must behave. He has the same power as a white man's judge or justice of the peace. He can fine the people if they don't obey the rules, and everybody knows the rules for they are old rules.

... If anything goes wrong, the Governor calls the Council together in his house to talk it over...

I told them that is the power of Self-Government.

### SOURCE 2:

From: 'It Didn't Pan Out as We Thought It Was Going To' Amos Owen on the Indian Reorganization Act. Amos Owen, a Sioux tribal chieftain, was interviewed by historian Herbert T Hoover in 1970.

**Owen:** Yes. It didn't pan out as we thought it was going to be. Of course, I was pretty young at the time, but I remember when we first organized, the Wheeler-Howard Act was I guess originally the way it was written up, it was really good. If the Indians made a little money or they became more prosperous as a community, they could, in turn, buy up more land. That was the way the Wheeler-Howard Act was written up. And before it went through Congress, I guess, it was revised a bit so that buying back land was struck out of some of the papers it was drawn up on. I don't know how this came about, but it wasn't in the charter and the constitution and bylaws when the thing came into effect. So we done it; I can't just go out and say the Bureau of Indian Affairs done it. But they didn't believe in colonies like ours, a small community like ours buying back land that originally belonged to us anyway.

## Simple essay style

Below is a sample exam question. Use your own knowledge and the information on the opposite page to produce a plan for this question. Choose four general points, and provide three pieces of specific information to support each general point. Once you have planned your essay, write the introduction and conclusion for the essay. The introduction should list the points to be discussed in the essay. The conclusion should summarise the key points and justify which point was the most important.

> To what extent did the New Deal successfully address the political, economic and social problems faced by Native Americans?

# The impact of the New Deal and war on Hispanic Americans

## Change for Hispanic Americans

### Depression and New Deal

The New Deal had had little positive impact on Hispanic Americans. Indeed, in the face of the Depression in 1931 a major deportation programme had begun that saw 400,000 Hispanic Americans deported to Mexico by 1935. These figures included many children who had been born in the USA and thereby acquired US citizenship but were deported with their parents.

Many southwestern states actually banned Hispanic Americans from local public work schemes during the New Deal, and numbers who traditionally migrated to California during harvest time found their opportunities diminished as unemployed migrants from other parts of the USA took what employment there was.

### New Deal Agencies

The WPA and other agencies employed Hispanic Americans on the same basis as members of other ethnic groups:

- the **Farm Security Administration** set up centres for those still employed in seasonal agriculture, for example, in the San Joachim Valley in California
- Comparatively few Hispanic Americans benefited from welfare programmes, however, or the Social Security Act because as transients, they lacked residency qualifications, or were living in the USA illegally. Moreover, the Act itself did not in its provisions include agricultural workers or domestic servants, which provided much employment for Hispanic Americans.

### The impact of war

In the war, Hispanic Americans found employment as readily as other ethnic groups. Around 500,000 joined the military. Another 17,000 found employment in the Los Angeles shipyards. These had employed none in 1941. From August 1942 the **bracero program** began, recruiting Mexicans to work in agriculture and railroads to meet the shortages of labour.

### Discrimination

Hispanic Americans often faced discrimination, for example in oil and copper companies in the southwest. The **State Department** vetoed a public enquiry because it felt this would discredit the USA in Mexico and provide good publicity for the enemies of the USA. Indeed, the FEPC, which had been investigating these allegations, was told to halt its enquiries.

### Zoot Suit Riots

Many Hispanic Americans favoured '**Zoot suits**', loosely hanging suits worn with lots of chains and jewellery. These came to be associated with lawless behaviour and immorality.

They also faced violence in Los Angeles in 1943 after clashes between naval recruits and gangs of 'Zoot suiters'. It was noted that the police treated the naval recruits far more leniently and blamed the Hispanic Americans for the trouble.

### Hispanic American women

Hispanic women had particularly been associated with either remaining at home or working in domestic service. However, the war brought the same opportunities for them as other groups of women. The greater independence these offered caused tension in many Hispanic families and led many males to rethink women's roles. Nevertheless, these opportunities were perceived as temporary until the war was over.

**Write the question**

The following sources relate to the treatment of Hispanic Americans on the Home Front during the Second World War. Use your own knowledge and read the guidance detailing what you need to know about Hispanic Americans during this period. Having done this, write an exam-style question using the sources.

How far could the historian make use of Sources 1 and 2 together to investigate...?

_____

_____

Explain your answer, using both sources, the information given about them and your own knowledge of the historical context.

When you have written a question, design a plan to answer it.

## SOURCE 1

From an article, published in *Common Ground* by journalist, George I. Sanchez offering the background to the June 1943 riots.

When the pachuco (name given to zoot-suiter) "crime wave" broke last year, I communicated with the Office of War Information: "I understand that a grand jury is looking into the 'Mexican' problem in Los Angeles and that there seems to be considerable misunderstanding as to the causes of the gang activities of Mexican youth in that area. I hear also that much ado is being made about 'Aztec forebears,' 'blood lust' and similar claptrap in interpreting the behavior of these citizens. It would be indeed unfortunate if this grand jury investigation were to go off on a tangent, witchhunting in anthropological antecedents for causes which, in reality, lie right under the noses of the public service agencies in Los Angeles County."

Subsequent developments have borne out the fears implied above. And still, in June of this year, the Los Angeles City Council could think of no better answer to the deep-rooted negligence of public service agencies than to deliberate over an ordinance outlawing zoot suits! The segregatory attitudes and practices, and the vicious economic exploitation directed against the "Mexican" in California in the past – not zoot suits – are responsible for the pachucos of today...

## SOURCE 2

From an article on the June 1943 'Zoot suit' riots by Al Waxman, editor of the *Eastside Journal*, an East Los Angeles community newspaper.

At Twelfth and Central I came upon a scene that will long live in my memory. Police were swinging clubs and servicemen were fighting with civilians. Wholesale arrests were being made by the officers.

Four boys came out of a pool hall. They were wearing the zoot-suits that have become the symbol of a fighting flag. Police ordered them into arrest cars. One refused. He asked: 'Why am I being arrested?' The police officer answered with three swift blows of the night-stick across the boy's head and he went down. As he sprawled, he was kicked in the face. Police had difficulty loading his body into the vehicle because he was one-legged and wore a wooden limb. Maybe the officer didn't know he was attacking a cripple...

Rushing back to the east side to make sure that things were quiet here, I came upon a band of servicemen making a systematic tour of East First Street. They had just come out of a cocktail bar where four men were nursing bruises. Three autos loaded with Los Angeles policemen were on the scene but the soldiers were not molested.

The New Deal and wartime years had profound social and cultural changes.

## WPA support for writers and musicians

The New Deal had encouraged the arts both to create employment and record what people saw as a significant era. The WPA was given funding to encourage writers and artists to record the Depression era.

The Federal Writers' Project (FWP) was set up under the auspices of the WPA to provide employment for authors. It compiled works of local and oral history, including 2,300 slave narratives and detailed guidebooks for each state explaining its specific history, culture and economy. At any one time, over 6,000 were at work in the FWP. In Indiana, for example, 150 were employed under this program. It was through their work that voices which otherwise would have been lost were recorded. The last remaining Native Americans who could remember their traditional nomadic plains lifestyle, for example, were interviewed before they died.

The Federal Music Project employed musicians to give concerts and hold festivals and also to document US music traditions, for example, rediscovering forgotten blues artists such as Son House. Members also worked in schools to develop musical education and gave instruction to adults.

## Tension in the Federal Music Project

Tensions within the Federal Music Project exemplified the debates about what the programmes were for. The Director, Dr Nikolai Sokoloff believed it was about promoting classical music, while his deputy Charles Seeger felt it was more about recording traditional music and making music more accessible to everyone – in keeping with the inclusive nature of the New Deal.

## The growing power of radio and popular music

Radio became possibly the most important source of up-to-date news during the war. Broadcasters acting as war correspondents such as Ed Morrow sent moving accounts of the London Blitz, which were influential in gaining US support for Britain. It was also used for propaganda with documentaries such as 'Lest We Forget' and 'You Can't Do Business with Hitler'.

### Popular music

Popular music played a vital role in maintaining morale both during the New Deal and wartime years. Songwriters were quick to latch on to key events such as 'Hats off to MacArthur' as General Douglas MacArthur led the campaign to keep control of the Philippines in 1942. Music also had a sentimental value, linking those at home with loved ones far away. Popular songs sometimes reminded those at home of the importance of faithfulness to partners on active service – for example, the Andrews Sisters singing, 'Don't sit under the apple tree with anyone else but me.' Patriotic tunes were very popular, especially 'God Bless America', first written in 1918, which became something of an anthem during the war years. Overall, however, music was evocative of home, playing on nostalgia and promoting the dream of a return to loved ones.

### Bobby Soxers

Many girls became known as 'bobby soxers'. They developed their own fashions and leisure activities revolving around cinema and dance. In particular they listened to swing music and one of its leading exponents, Frank Sinatra, became effectively the first teenage idol.

**Developing an argument**

Below are a sample exam question, a list of key points to be made in the essay, and a paragraph from the essay. Read the question, the plan, and the sample paragraph. Rewrite the paragraph in order to develop an argument. Your paragraph should answer the question directly, and set out the evidence that supports your argument. Crucially, it should develop an argument by setting out a general answer to the question and reasons that support this.

How far do you agree that American culture was transformed in the years 1933–45?

Key points:
- The New Deal had encouraged the arts both to create employment and record life during the 1930s.
- The Federal Writers' Project recorded local and oral history and captured accounts of slavery and nomadic Native American life before all who could remember them died.
- Radio was the most important form of media to keep people informed during wartime.
- Popular music had an important impact in linking those serving abroad with their loved ones at home.

> The New Deal and war years saw important developments in culture. The New Deal itself encouraged the arts. The WPA supported the Federal Writers' Project, which recorded oral testimonies of former slaves and members of different ethnic groups and produced valuable guidebooks to the different states. US traditions and folklore were recorded. During the war, radio was important in keeping people aware of news. Popular music linked servicemen with their loved ones at home. Some songs highlighted the fears of cheating on partners.

 **The flaw in the argument**                                                                                          **a**

Below are a sample exam question and a paragraph written in answer to this question. The paragraph contains an argument which attempts to answer the question. However, there is an error in the argument. Use your knowledge of this topic to identify the flaw in the argument.

'Popular music and radio became particularly important in uniting Americans during the war years.' How far do you agree with this statement?

> Radio and popular music served to unite the nation during the war years. Radio was probably the most common form of information and stations sent correspondents to war zones to report on events. It was influential too: Ed Morrow's reports from Britain during the Blitz led to greater support for Britain. Music also kept people connected – the knowledge that loved ones overseas may be listening to the same songs was a comfort. However, it also warned them to remain loyal to their partners – 'Don't sit under the apple tree with anyone else but me'.

# Wartime domestic propaganda

The entertainment industry was strongly geared to the war effort and patriotic propaganda during the war years.

## The power of Hollywood

Hollywood responded enthusiastically to the war effort producing both propaganda films and escapism. While many actors such as James Stewart served with distinction in the armed forces, others sold war bonds in massive campaigns and entertained the troops, often in war zones. Many worked in the Hollywood Canteen, which was established by film star Bette Davis to provide free meals and entertainment for lonely servicemen.

## War bonds

War bonds were loans raised by the government to help pay for the war. They were bought by ordinary people and were to be repaid after 10 years at an interest rate of 2.9 per cent. Many celebrities went on nationwide tours to sell them. The comedy actress Dorothy Lamour sold $350 million of them. In September 1942 a 'bond blitz' realised more than $800 million after 300 actors had worked 18-hour days to promote them. Decorated war heroes were also very successful in selling them.

The buying of war bonds became a significant way in which ordinary people could show they were making a contribution to victory.

## War films

The Office of War Entertainment was set up in 1942 to co-ordinate efforts to film and record wartime activities. Many famous directors made training movies and morale-boosting documentaries, such as John Huston's *Return to the Aleutians* (1945), or propaganda documentaries, such as Frank Capra's series *Why We Fight* (1942–45). War movies were often realistic – their audiences of military personnel or their relatives at home could no longer be patronised by the message that war was chivalrous and noble even if the cause was just. Some like *Guadacanal Diary* (1943) had the feel of documentaries. Even so the aim was to engender patriotism and support for the war.

## The rise of Disney

Disney studios had risen as the main producers of cartoon and animated films and enjoyed huge success during the 1930s. During the war, Disney became important in the production of propaganda and training films. They were taken over by the military and 90 per cent of its workforce became involved in war-related film production. Disney characters were also used in films to improve morale: Donald Duck appeared in *Der Fuhrer's Face*, which ridiculed Hitler and won an Oscar for best animated film in 1943.

## Escapism

Movies were also important for escapism purposes. Musicals were popular, particularly if they featured glamorous singers and dancers like Betty Gable. Popular comedians included Abbot and Costello and Bob Hope. There was also an understandable market for nostalgia with sentimental films such as *Meet Me in St Louis* (1944) portraying an imagined halcyon past. The problems of the Home Front were also depicted, often in humorous style with the need to be vigilant against Nazi spies in *My Favorite Blonde* (1942) and the housing shortages in *The More the Merrier* (1943). Perhaps the greatest evocation of the war as a worthwhile moral crusade was in *Casablanca* (1942) with the Nazis depicted as an evil that must be defeated.

# (i) You're the examiner    **a**

Below are a sample A Level exam question and a paragraph written in answer to this question. Read the paragraph and the mark scheme provided on page 104. Decide which level you would award the paragraph and give a justification for your choice.

How far could the historian make use of Sources 1 and 2 together to investigate the impact of propaganda on the mobilisation of the American Home Front in the period 1941–45? Explain your answer, using both sources, the information given about them and your own knowledge of the historical context.

Both sources are useful in showing the impact of propaganda to galvanise the Home Front in the USA during the Second World War using popular media. The first source shows how geared up Hollywood was to fund raising and the promotion of war bonds, while the second is a humorous reminder of the need for rationing by poking fun at a character who disagrees with it. The second source is more immediate having been transmitted at the time on the radio, which was the most common media by which messages were communicated nationally. The first is a memoir written twenty years after the event although it does capture the intense fund raising activities in Hollywood, and shows that it was difficult to opt out. Both sources therefore infer the comprehensive nature of the efforts required. People couldn't exclude themselves.

## SOURCE 1

From *Inquisition in Eden,* a 1965 memoir by Alvin Bessie, a screenwriter for Warner Brothers films during the war. He had left-wing politics and was later imprisoned for refusing to testify about his role in the Communist party.

No week passed without its drive: for British War Relief, Russian War relief, the Red Cross, the Salvation Army and the Blood Bank (which was almost a permanent institution on the lot) ... Bond drives always received enormous support, for war bonds were an excellent investment, and there was no one who did not pick up a $25 or $50 bond at least once a week...

There was a huge rally for the Red Cross that was held on one of our largest sound stages, and while attendance was not exactly compulsory, your absence would have been noted by the captains in charge of each department of the studio... There were stars who made speeches, and Major Richard Bong, the ace of the Pacific Theater of Operations, made a brief appearance... and a great deal of money was raised.

## SOURCE 2

Extract from a popular comedy radio series *Fibber McGee and Molly*, with the purpose of entertaining and boosting morale during the war years.

**Fibber McGee**: This mileage rationing has got me disgusted.

**Molly**: You know, he's been raving about it all day, Mr. Wilcox. He thinks the O-P-A is trying to make an A-P-E out of him.

**McGee**: And they are, too. A citizen of my standing trying to get along on an AAA book—it's a lot of foolishness. I've got business to take care of!

**Wilcox**: What business, pal?

**McGee**: Well, in the first place, I—Well, gee whiz. I've got responsibilities.

**Molly**: Oh, he really has, Mr. Wilcox.

**McGee**: Yeah.

**Molly**: You know, he's the sole support of three pinochle players at the Elk's Club.

**Wilcox**: Fibber, you talk like a chump!

**McGee**: Huh?

**Wilcox**: Yes. Mileage rationing is the only fair way to cut down nonessential driving. When the rubber this country has got is gone, it's gone. That's all there is. There isn't any more.

**McGee**: Well, then they should have foreseen that and took care of the situation.

**Molly**: Well, everybody can't be as farsighted as you are, dearie.

During the war years US industries produced more war materiel than all of its enemies put together. Between 1941 and 1945 the USA produced 86,000 tanks, 290,000 aircraft and 15 million rifles. Farm incomes grew by 250 per cent – problems of overproduction were negated as the USA became a principal food supplier to allies and countries dislocated by war.

## The collapse of unemployment

The USA reached full employment by 1942, after which unemployment figures became insignificant – 1.2 per cent by 1944.

By 1943 there were labour shortages. As a result:
- women joined the workforce in increasing numbers – 6.5 million in 1944
- black people also found plentiful employment. The numbers of black Americans working for federal government rose from 50,000 in 1939 to 200,000 by 1944.

## Women and the war effort

### Role and status of women

The war significantly affected the role and status of women.
- Many faced huge problems having to juggle childcare with long working hours.
- There was in particular a shortage of housing in urban areas and many families faced overcrowding and cramped conditions.
- Women also faced shortages of materials deployed for the war effort. They grew their own produce in 'Victory gardens', joined the Women's Land Army to replace male agricultural workers, and learned to manage without luxuries.
- To accommodate the growing numbers of women in war work, the Community Facilities Act of 1941 provided childcare facilities for women in defence plants. However, demand was far in excess of supply.

Table 3.1 Numbers of Women Workers 1941–44

| Year | Total | % of women in the manufacturing workforce |
|------|-------|-------------------------------------------|
| 1941 | 14,600,000 | 22 % |
| 1944 | 19,370,000 | 32% |

## Women and employment

Women found plentiful employment during the war, although they faced discrimination, including lower pay. While the Fair Employment Practices Commission (FEPC, see page 58) addressed the latter it could not enforce equal pay. Labour unions were unsympathetic because they expected women to leave paid employment after hostilities ended and return to their homecare and child-rearing duties. While they were enthusiastically recruited for the duration, few expected the growth in female employment to be permanent. Indeed, the United Electrical Workers' Union was one of the few which did campaign for equal pay. However, by the time the War Labor Board accepted its arguments, the hostilities were over and the campaign was dropped as war conditions no longer applied.

Nevertheless, the media made much of women workers for propaganda purposes. One particular icon was Rosie the Riveter, a cartoon character based on a popular song from 1942 that encouraged women to take up war work. By January 1942, the director of the Women's Bureau reported that 2,800,000 women were involved in war work. By 1945 300,000 had joined the female branches of the armed forces although they were not involved in combat.

## The contribution of young people

Young people contributed fully to the war effort. They became increasingly involved in paid employment to replace those in the military: 66 per cent of teenage boys found jobs. In 1940, 900,000 14 to 18 year olds were employed, a figure which rose to over 3 million by 1944. Many states altered their child labour laws accordingly.

Widespread employment did lead to problems:
- with fathers largely absent and a ready supply of income, many were accused of disrespect for their elders and unsocial behaviour
- some joined gangs such as 'Zoot suiters' and were blamed for increases in crime.

It should be remembered, however, that most teenage boys were only in paid employment until conscripted into the armed forces, normally at the age of 18.

## Establish criteria

Below is a sample exam question, which requires you to make a judgement. The key term in the question has been underlined. Defining the meaning of the key term can help you establish criteria that you can use to make a judgement.

Read the question, define the key term and then set out two or three criteria based on the key term, which you can use to reach and justify a judgement.

How accurate is it to say that the economy of the USA was <u>transformed</u> during the years 1941–45?

Definition:

_____

_____

Criteria to judge the extent to which the economy of the USA was transformed during the years 1941–45:

_____

## Reach a judgement

Having defined the key term and established a series of criteria, you should now make a judgement.

Consider how far the economy was transformed during the years 1941–45. Summarise your judgements below:

● Criterion 1:

_____

_____

Finally, sum up your judgement.

Based on the criteria, how accurate is it to say that the economy of the USA was transformed during the years 1941–45?

_____

_____

_____

Tip: remember you should weigh up evidence of transformation against evidence of continuity in your conclusion.

# The impact of war on the USA

The war had a dramatic impact on the USA, with unprecedented levels of control as the entire country was mobilised for war.

## Migration to urban and rural centres

Estimates suggest that 27 million Americans moved during the war. As a result, the population of rural areas fell by 29 per cent. Most moved to areas with defence plants, such as California, where the population rose by 72 per cent during the war years. Around 200,000 moved to government employment in Washington DC. Throughout the USA there were huge housing shortages: one solution was to build barrack-style accommodation which at one time housed 1.5 million people.

## Dislocation

The demands of wartime inevitably led to considerable dislocation. Fifteen million served in the military, many overseas. Their absence led to a growth in the divorce rate, and youth crime. The population, however, increased, notably in the '**furlough babies**' conceived during periods of leave.

## New industries

The war saw the development of new industries such as advanced electronics, synthetic materials and pharmaceuticals. By 1945 the USA was the world's biggest exporter of synthetic rubber. It also pioneered the mass production of penicillin, which saved the lives of millions of wounded Allied soldiers.

## Growing power of trade unions

The war years saw huge rises in labour union membership – from 10.5 million in 1940 to 14.75 million in 1945. The main unions agreed to take industrial disputes to a National War Labor Board: however, the war years did see considerable industrial unrest – in 1943 400,000 coal miners struck for higher wages. In response, in June 1943 the Smith–Connally War Disputes Act allowed federal government to take control of any essential industries faced with industrial action. This was an example of growing government intervention, which was a feature of wartime USA.

## The growth of the Military-Industrial Complex

The most significant industrial growth was in armaments. The switch to armaments production came relatively easily because so many industrial plants were idle in 1940 – as early as 1941, 33 per cent of US production was devoted to war production. As the war developed, armaments production became more specialised and focused, especially in particular areas – for example, California, the South and the Far West. Inevitably, this infrastructure remained intact in the post-war years – many desert areas, for example, became associated with weapons testing because they were relatively uninhabited. People spoke of a **military-industrial complex**, meaning the links between industry and the military, which was to become especially significant in the post-war years.

**Support your judgement**

Below are a sample exam question and two basic judgements. Read the exam question and the two judgements. Support the judgement that you agree with more strongly by adding a reason that justifies the judgement.

'The lives of many people on the Home Front transformed during the years 1941–45.' How far do you agree with this statement?

Overall, many people's lives on the Home Front had been transformed during the years 1941–45

_____

_____

Overall, many people's lives were little changed by developments on the Home Front between 1941 and 1945

_____

_____

Tip: whichever option you choose you will have to weigh up both sides of the argument. You could use phrases such as 'whereas' or words like 'although' in order to help the process of evaluation.

 **Recommended reading**

- Ronald Allen Goldberg, *America in the Forties*, Chapter 2 (2012)
- Ronald Takaki, *Double Victory: A Multicultural History of America in the Second World War* (2000)
- John Morton Blum, *V was for Victory: Politics and Culture during World War Two*, pages 90–140, 192–221 (1976)

On pages 73–75 are sample exam answers to the questions on these two pages. Read the answers and the comments around them.

How much weight do you give the evidence of Source 2 for an enquiry into relations between white and black Americans in the USA during the Second World War? Explain your answer using the source, the information given about it and your own knowledge of the historical context. **AS**

How far could the historian make use of Sources 1 and 2 together to investigate the treatment of black Americans in the workplace during the Second World War? Explain your answer using the source, the information given about it and your own knowledge of the historical context.

## SOURCE 1

From Executive Order 8802, June 1941 banning discrimination in the defence industry where there was a need for workers; the Order went on to set up the Fair Employment Practices Committee.

Whereas there is evidence that available and needed workers have been barred from employment in industries engaged in defence solely because of considerations of race, creed, color or national origin, to the detriment of workers' morale and of national unity:

Now therefore by virtue of the authority vested in me by the Constitution and the statutes and as a pre-requisite to the successful conduct of our defence production effort, I do hereby reaffirm the policy of the United States that there shall be no discrimination in employing workers in defence industries because of race, creed, color or national origin and I do hereby declare it is the duty of employers to provide for the full and equitable participation of all workers in defence industries without discrimination.

## SOURCE 2

From Malcolm X, *The Autobiography of Malcolm X*, published in 1965. Malcolm X was a young man growing up in wartime New York. Malcolm here is visiting an Induction centre psychiatrist seeking to avoid the draft. He did subsequently avoid conscription and later became an important black American nationalist.

The receptionist there was a Negro nurse. I remember she was in her early twenties, not bad to look at. She was one of the Negro 'firsts'.

Negroes know what I'm talking about. Back then, the white man during the war was so pressed for personnel that he began letting some Negroes put down their buckets and mops and dust rags and use a pencil, or sit at some desk, or hold some twenty-five cent title. You couldn't read the negro press for the big pictures of the smug black 'firsts'....

When, finally a buzz came at her desk, she didn't send me in, she went in. I knew what she was doing, she was going to make clear in advance what she thought of me. This is still one of the black man's big troubles today. So many of the so-called 'upper class' negroes are so busy trying to impress the white man that they are 'different from those others' that they can't see they are only helping the white man to keep his low opinion of all Negroes.

Below is the model answer to the AS Level question.

This source has partial weight in an enquiry into the relations between white and black American during World War Two. As it is written by a black nationalist who was hoping to avoid conscription into the armed forces, it does contain an element of cynicism. The writer will almost certainly be critical. It is moreover only one person's view. However, one example could stand for many, and one account could be typical of many. The writer is attempting to convey general truths about race relations from this specific experience.

*Introduction confidently summarises points to be made.*

The argument the writer is putting forward is that many black Americans tried to impress whites with a sense of superiority over other blacks, and this in fact only reinforced the white's low opinion of black Americans. Malcolm X does this by suggesting the receptionist is going to share her poor impression of him with the white psychiatrist before he had even seen him. However, this is conjecture; he has no evidence, simply suspicion deployed to reinforce his existing belief. – which is not to say he is incorrect. Malcolm X indeed assumes his audience agrees, that he is speaking well known truths they will recognise – 'Negroes know what I'm talking about'.

*Valid criticism of the argument.*

The tone of the extract is dismissive. That the writer distrusts the process of recruitment of black Americans to more responsible positions is highlighted by the comments, 'put down their buckets and mops and dust rags and use a pencil, or sit at some desk, or hold some twenty-five cent title', implying they would previously have held menial posts and these promotions were giving them an inflated sense of self-importance. However Malcolm X betrays his own prejudices, saying for example that the receptionist was 'not bad to look at' which can be seen as a denigration even with the existing sexist attitudes towards women of the period. Undoubtedly the war did create more employment opportunities for women, and many black women did benefit from these. However one cannot surmise as does Malcolm X that these women – or indeed other blacks promoted during wartime – are almost collaborators with their white superiors to keep other black people in their place.

*Valid discussion of tone, although quote is rather long.*

*Excellent critical engagement with argument.*

To offer more weight, more instances would need to be offered. Malcolm X attempts to generalise from one example and even that is based on speculation. His general point that blacks are collaborating in their own denigration may have value but cannot be inferred from one example. The source has value in showing the opinion of one black nationalist – but it is important to consider that it may have been deployed to confirm what he already believed, and more evidence is needed.

*Summary of limitation in valid conclusion.*

In taking a critical view of the weight, the candidate shows the confidence to discuss the source limitations while acknowledging where it is useful. There is critical engagement and the differences between information and opinion are clearly discussed. There is some consideration of context and the need to interpret source material from the context of the values of the time. The concluding judgement is valid. This would achieve a high Level 4 mark.

## Consolidation (sources)

These answers demand a combination of argument, own knowledge and reference to sources. Colour code each of these three components.

Below is a model answer to the A Level question on page 72.

Both sources are partially useful to an historian investigating the treatment of black Americans in the workplace during the Second World War, although both also have limitations. The first source is an official document outlining federal government policy; it tells us little of its impact, while the second source is one person's opinion based more on conjecture than fact. However, within the historical context, both are useful in that the first outlines government policy to afford fair treatment to black Americans, while the second from Malcolm X outlines one person's experience and opinions. One then deals with theory and the other with practice.

Source 1 is a formal response to racial discrimination, setting out the case that federal government policy opposes discrimination. It also makes the point that it is the duty of employers to ensure discrimination does not occur. Source 2 on the other hand is one person's opinion. Malcolm X, a black nationalist, is more cynical in discussing the practice of the black American experience in wartime by arguing that some have been promoted as a result of labour shortages during the war, but then goes on to make a wider case about the attitudes of many of those who were promoted in this way. His purpose is therefore different to the authors of Source 1. Malcolm X, moreover, implies agreement on the part of his audience – 'Negroes know what I'm talking about', suggesting indeed that the point he is making will be well known to fellow black Americans.

In some ways, while the sources appear different, they do agree with each other, particularly in terms of implication. Source 1 is reaffirming a policy of non-discrimination therefore acknowledging not only that discrimination has taken place but implying that previous pronouncements against it must have had little effect. Malcolm X on the other hand is implying black people have only been given less menial jobs because of the exigencies of wartime; 'Back then the white man during the war was so pressed for personnel that he began letting some negroes put down their buckets and mops and dust rags and use a pencil...' He goes on to suggest that these beneficiaries try to win the approval of their white bosses by denigrating other blacks. Here he asserts the receptionist has gone to warn the white psychiatrist about him, and warns that such behaviour only serves to reinforce whites' low impression of black Americans. However, the utility of the source has to be questioned. Malcolm X is basing his argument on what he believes is happening; he has no evidence this is the case.

In this sense Source 2 offers an opinion, although it may well be based on what Malcolm X knows about lives of black Americans. Source 1 meanwhile implies that discrimination is rife but offers no concrete evidence in support beyond the telling need for 'reassertion' referred to earlier. However, we know from the historic context that discrimination was rife. Executive Order 8802 indeed was an official response to the threatened 1941 march on Washington to protest discrimination in workplaces. The argument in Source 1 is sound. Given that more workers were needed, irrespective of race, it would be illogical to refuse them in terms of ethnicity. Malcolm X, of course, agreed with the need. He asserts that more blacks are being given more responsible positions because of the need as a result of the war and in this sense his views agree with the intention expressed in Source 1.

**Margin annotations:**

Introduction summarises the issues to be discussed.

Sources are described but could be considered more together.

Comment could be developed here.

This point could be developed – as it stands more of an assertion than an argument.

Valid inferences. Valid point but could be developed elsewhere in the essay.

Valid context.

Paragraph contains diverse points. All are valid but might have been better to have developed in separate paragraphs.

Both sources have limitations in terms of usefulness. The first source asserts a position. It affirms that discrimination is wrong, and that it is the responsibility of employers to combat it. Source 2 implies that blacks are only being promoted as result of the wartime need and let their race down by trying to win approval of their white bosses by criticising other blacks – a sort of 'divide and rule' by whites. However, it is important to reassert that this is one man's opinion – and he himself denigrates to a certain extent by suggesting completely unnecessarily in terms of his argument that the receptionist 'wasn't bad to look at'. This sexist comment may have reflected common attitudes of the period. Of course discrimination against blacks was common too, and Source 1 offers no sanctions against its continuation. It simply asserts it is the role of employers to prevent it.

> Not sure of relevance here.
> Valid points but structurally rather awkward.

Overall, both sources are then partially useful. While Source 1 states an official position from the time, Source 2 offers a stance. Neither offer concrete supporting evidence, although both imply discrimination is taking place albeit in different ways – the Executive Order needing to reaffirm the federal government position and the black nationalist asserting that blacks have only been promoted because of the wartime needs, and indeed how their behaviour reaffirms whites' low opinions of them.

> Valid judgement but could have more in support.

**Sufficient and relevant knowledge to tackle most aspects of the question. However, at times there is a lack of precision and while overall the structure is sound, there are times when it is rather awkward. At times the sources are considered separately; this cannot always be avoided and will not necessarily lose marks as long as they are in the main considered together. The overall judgement could be better supported. This response would be marked at Level 4 rather than 5.**

### Moving from a Level 4 to Level 5

The exam focus essay at the end of Section One (pages 27–28) provided a Level 5 essay. The A Level essay here achieves a Level 4. Read both essays, and the comments provided. Make a list of the additional features required to push a Level 4 essay into Level 5.

# 4 The transformation of the USA, 1945–54

## Economic transformation

The post-war period saw the development of a period of prosperity in the USA unprecedented in history in its range and longevity. By 1945, the USA with seven per cent of the world's population enjoyed 42 per cent of its wealth. Per capita income at $1,450 was twice as high as that of Britain, one of its closest competitors. GNP had risen 35 per cent since 1941. Economic expansion led to greater employment opportunities for more of the population and a huge growth in **consumerism**. However, not all areas of the USA were equally prosperous.

### Government policies to encourage growth

The government encouraged economic growth in a variety of ways:
- in 1944 Roosevelt had proposed an 'Economic Bill of Rights' committing the Federal Government to issues such as full employment and adequate welfare provision
- in 1946 the Employment Act formalised the quest for full employment. However, the demand for labour was so high that the new law was unnecessary.

### Development of the Cold War

An economic boom was fuelled in part by the development of the **Cold War** and continued need for military spending, but it was also important as a result of the need to stimulate trade and help countries recover from war. **Marshall Aid,** for example, saw $13 million given to western European countries; much of this was used to purchase US goods so in a sense the USA received back many of these funds.

### The GI Bill of Rights

The GI Bill of Rights (also known as the Selective Servicemen's Readjustment Act) was passed in 1944.
- It offered grants to ex-servicemen for education or to set up businesses. Eight million took up the offer.
- Its provisions were administered by the **Veterans' Association**.
- One provision was largely unnecessary: veterans were awarded $20 per week while looking for work: less than 20 per cent of the monies allocated for this were distributed because work was so plentiful to come by.
- It offered home loans to facilitate home ownership. Mortgages were available of up to 90 per cent of the cost, with interest rates as low as four per cent. Almost 2.4 million veterans took advantage of this, a significant factor in the development of widespread home ownership.

### Growing mobility

The growth of car ownership led to much greater mobility. Sales of new cars rose from 69,500 in 1945 to 6.7 million by 1950 – and most were US made. In 1950 there were only 16,000 foreign cars in the USA. While the market was still dominated by the '**Big three**', there was plenty of choice – 350 different models by 1961. Also, the number of two-car families doubled between 1951 and 1958.

### Roadbuilding

The increase in mobility led to the development of roadside hotels, garages and gas stations. The first Holiday Inn opened in 1952.

## Select the detail

Below is a sample exam question with the accompanying sources. Having read the question and the sources, complete the following activity.

How far could the historian make use of Sources 1 and 2 together to investigate the extent of prosperity in the USA in the post-war period to the early 1950s?

Below are three claims that you could make when answering the question. Read the claims and then select quotes from the sources to support them. Remember to keep the quotes short; never copy more than a sentence.

1 Prosperity was unevenly distributed across the USA

2 There was a large demand for cars after the war

3 Source 2 is valuable to an historian as it gives an alternative view to that of post-war prosperity in the USA because...

## SOURCE 1

Extract from *The Big Change: America Transforms Itself,* by Frederick Lewis Allen, 1952. Allen was a journalist specialising in the early to mid-twentieth century development of the USA, famous for his work, *Only Yesterday* (see page 26).

... The war induced prosperity was speeding structural change on a quite different level. The jingle of cash in the pocket was preparing innumerable ordinary Americans to buy and use more machines just as soon as these became available. And after V J day (the end of the war with Japan) the rush was on.

Everybody, to begin with, seemed to want new automobiles, which had been unavailable for purchasing during the war. There was hot competition for the joy of getting a new car fresh from the assembly line; people talked about the number of years they had 'had their name in' with dealers; there was a lively racket in ostensibly used cars; and it was years before the automobile manufacturers could catch up with the demand. After they had done so, in the single year 1950 they sold more than eight million vehicles – which was more cars than had existed in the entire United States at the end of World War 1.

## SOURCE 2

From *Inside USA,* by John Gunther, published in 1947. Gunther was a well-respected and authoritative journalist.

Georgia is a state with some statistics to unnerve anybody... there are 488,711 homes without running water... Georgia has the highest syphilis among whites in the Union with an average of 145.9 cases per 1,000 as opposed to 4.8 for New Hampshire... only 170 out of... towns have a public sewer system, and... in a recent three-year period there were 3,000 cases of typhus, a disease almost unknown to civilised communities, and spread by the fleas from rats.

... Farmers in the North got silos, hybrid corn and mechanization: those in the South got pellagra, hookworm and malaria.

The first thing I noticed was the outdoor privy... There is no running water or electricity; an old bedspring leans against a rotting tree; an iron pot – the laundry – sits shakily on burnt stones. We moved on to the house which is propped up on lumps of rock; if you step firmly on the 'veranda' the gray mouldering boards give way.

# The new consumer society

The growth in home ownership and increasing confidence that prosperity was here to stay led to a dramatic growth in consumerism. During the 1950s the average family's disposable income rose by an average 17 per cent, much of which was spent on consumer goods.

## Home ownership

House construction expanded rapidly in the post-war years. In 1944, 114,000 family homes were built: in 1950 this figure had risen to 15 million. The percentage of Americans owning their own homes rose from 50 to 60 per cent between 1950 and 1960. Homes were filled with consumer items – household appliances, modern furniture and ornamental goods. Home ownership came to symbolise the prosperity of ordinary Americans.

## The growth of the suburbs

Many new homes were in suburbs on the outskirts of urban areas. This meant that many Americans gained space in their homes – space for gardens, garages and above all, privacy.

The numbers living here grew from 17 per cent in 1920 to 33 per cent by 1960. Critics complained they lacked variety, but they did see new developments such as **shopping malls** – these grew from eight in 1946 to over 4,000 by the late 1950s.

As a result of suburbanisation the populations of big cities declined. As people left and the amount of tax revenue fell, urban areas frequently had to reduce the provision and quality of facilities such as schools and libraries. Inner city centres in particular became associated with less affluence and poor facilities.

## Levittown projects

Among the most famous of suburban houses were 'Levitt houses' built by William Levitt. These were **prefabricated** constructions, made from 27 standardised parts that were assembled on site. Levitt's first project was constructed in Long Island. By 1951 there were 17,000 Levitt homes accommodating 82,000 people. Because Levitt houses were mass produced, they were significantly cheaper than houses built by more traditional methods. Indeed, Levitt homes were available from $7,900, whereas the cheapest traditional homes began at around $8,450.

Levitt homes were only for whites, however. In 1955 none had been sold to black Americans.

## The growth of consumer society

During the post-war period there was a rapid expansion in consumer spending fuelled by incessant advertising, particularly on television – and the percentage of TV sets in homes grew from 0.4 per cent in 1947 to 55.7 per cent by 1954.

People were far more likely than their parents to stay home. Indeed, during the 1950s cinema and restaurant visits fell dramatically. Affluent consumers spent their money on new domestic appliances including television, and **white goods**. Indeed, by 1951, 90 per cent of US families had fridges and 75 per cent had washing machines and telephones.

As before, many of these goods were purchased on credit – the amount of debt increased from $5.7 billion in 1945 to $56.1 billion by 1960. By 1955 total household debt was 47 per cent relative to total disposable income.

Staying at home watching TV led to the development of frozen and convenience food, while the desire for convenience generally led to items as diverse as polaroid cameras and synthetic, easy-care fabrics.

### Extent of consumption

In the early 1950s the USA had six per cent of the world's population but consumed 33 per cent of all its goods. The average American had a lifestyle his or her parents could hardly have dreamed of. Nevertheless, it should be remembered that not all groups or regions shared in this prosperity.

Table 3.2 Regional differences in wealth in 1945

| State | Per capita income ($) |
|---|---|
| Alabama | 700 |
| California | 1,480 |
| Kentucky | 735 |
| Massachusetts | 1,321 |
| New Mexico | 1812 |
| South Carolina | 663 |

The table shows that *per capita* in Southern states was noticeably less than those of the North (Massachusetts) and West (California and New Mexico).

## Spot the inference   a

High-level answers avoid excessive summarising or paraphrasing the sources. Instead they make inferences from the sources, as well as analysing their value in terms of their context.

Below are a source and a series of statements. Read the source and decide which of the statements:

- makes inferences from the source (I)
- paraphrase the source (P)
- summarises the source (S)
- cannot be justified from the source (X)

Fill in the boxes below with either I, P, S, or X: ☐

- The USA was the richest country in the world. ☐
- The USA was rich overall but there were deep pockets of poverty ☐
- The USA spent much of its wealth on luxuries and trivia but didn't allocate money for important issues like cancer research ☐
- Everyone in the USA was free to spend their income as they chose. ☐

## SOURCE 1

From John Gunther, *Inside USA*, written in 1947. Gunther was an authoritative and well respected journalist.

The United States... contains four-fifths of the world's automobiles and one-half of its telephones... This country sells 70 million dollars' worth of cosmetics in a normal year, and kills forty thousand in automobile accidents...The United States consumed 1,115,000,000 quarts of ice cream last year and 660,000,000 doughnuts. Ninety-five million Americans go to the movies every week, and 55 million copies of pulp magazines are sold each month...

The United States is statistically the richest country in the world. It is also a country with no national unemployment or health insurance. Nothing in fact could be easier to list than some of our more preposterous and flamboyant contradictions:

In 1945 Americans spent $1,306,514,314 on race tracks... In 1946 a bill to appropriate 100 million dollars for cancer research was defeated in the House of Representatives.

The national income as reported last year was 159 billion dollars... But only one American family in thirty-four had an income of $7,500 a year or more, only one in ten had $4,000 and, more than 50 per cent had less than $122.00 per month.

## The flaw in the argument   a

Below are a sample exam question and a paragraph written in answer to this question. The paragraph contains an argument, which attempts to answer the question. However, there is an error in the argument. Use your knowledge of this topic to identify the flaw in the argument.

How accurate is it to say that in the early 1950s the USA enjoyed unprecedented prosperity?

The early 1950s saw the USA develop as by far the richest nation on earth. By 1945, the USA with seven per cent of the world's population enjoyed 42 per cent of its wealth. Per capita income at $1,450 was twice as high as that of Britain, one of its closest competitors. GNP had risen 35 per cent since 1945. By almost every criterion, the USA enjoyed unparalleled prosperity. By 1950, sales of new cars had risen to 6.7 million, while house ownership stood at over 50 per cent. It was a golden age for families. The divorce rate fell from 17.9 per 1,000 in 1946 to 9.6 by 1953, with the age of marriage falling for females to 20.5 years by 1956. Most brides quickly became pregnant to produce the so-called baby boom.

# The end of post-war euphoria

While Americans seemed happier and more confident in the post-war period, they were also more worried and fearful about the future because of the Cold War. This particularly manifested itself at home in terms of a further 'Red Scare' and anti-Communist crusade.

## House Un-American Activities Committee (HUAC)

US governments had long opposed Communism, which they saw as a threat to their way of life. **HUAC** meanwhile was a Congressional Committee that had been set up in 1938 to investigate what were perceived as threats to US values. Its original role was to investigate Nazi infiltration but by the mid-1940s it had turned its attention to Communists and their sympathisers.

- HUAC investigated Hollywood and pro-Communist material in films. Members feared pro-Communist content was being deployed to brainwash cinemagoers. Among those singled out for criticism was Charlie Chaplin, a British citizen who was forced to leave the USA. They ruined the careers of the Hollywood Ten, a group of writers and directors who refused to testify before HUAC. In 1954, a second investigation produced a 'blacklist' of 350 individuals who could not be employed in the film industry.
- HUAC also investigated labour unions and their links to Communism: by the terms of the 1946 Taft-Hartley Act leaders were forced to swear they were anti-Communist.
- They investigated the State Department, which they felt was infiltrated by spies. In 1947 the Loyalty Review Board was set up to investigate all government employees: within four years at least 4,000 had been dismissed accused of harbouring Communist sympathies.

This led to a second Red Scare, where as a result of the HUAC investigations, McCarthyism (see below), media focus and spy scandals (see page 82) people became increasingly afraid of Communist infiltration.

## McCarthyism and its impact

Joseph McCarthy was a Wisconsin Senator who in 1950 accused the State Department of being infested with 200 spies. Although he had no evidence to support his claims, this initiated a witch-hunt against public officials, which culminated in an investigation of the armed forces. One of McCarthy's investigative techniques was the use of 'multiple untruth' by which his accusations were so complex it was difficult to refute them coherently. McCarthy also had access to FBI files. He gained considerable support:

- from members of HUAC
- from conservatives who were suspicious of new ideas
- from church groups who associated Communism with the work of the Devil
- from less well educated and affluent members of society, many of whom were susceptible to conspiracy theories.

While McCarthy was successful at first in the widespread galvanising of public opinion, he lost credibility when his hearings were televised and viewers saw his drunken, bullying tactics. In tackling the army, which was embroiled in the **Korean War** fighting against Communist forces moreover, he lost significant support. Indeed, McCarthy himself became implicated in scandal when he deferred military conscription for members of his own staff.

McCarthy was criticised by President **Eisenhower** for his attack on the army, censured by the Senate and drifted back into obscurity before dying of alcoholism in 1957 – but at its height, his committee had been popular and such were the levels of fear that millions were prepared to believe his accusations.

## The impact of the second Red Scare

Fearing they would be accused of support for Communism, organisations such as the **National Association for the Advancement of Colored People (NAACP)** (see page 22) purged their membership of Communist sympathisers. Hundreds of ordinary people, especially in education were fired from their jobs for suspected Communist sympathies. Libraries were purged of books which could be read as pro-Communist – including in one case a book about Robin Hood.

**Add the context**

Below is a sample A Level exam question with the accompanying sources. Having read the question and the sources, complete the following activity.

How far could the historian make use of Sources 1 and 2 together to investigate the fall of Joseph McCarthy?

First, look for aspects of the source that refer to the events and discussion that were going on around the time that the source was written. Underline the key phrases and write a brief description of the context in the margin next to the source. Draw an arrow from the key phrase to the context. Try to find three key phrases in each source.

Tip: look at the information above the source – you should contextualise this too.

## SOURCE 1

Extract from *The Unquiet years: USA 1945 to 1955,* written by Hebert Agar (1957). Agar was a respected US journalist who supported ordinary people against unfair government practices.

His combination of rudeness, noise, threats and effrontery was accepted by his half-stunned associates until he proved himself an even greater threat to President Eisenhower than he had been to Truman. Then at last the Senate acted, and McCarthy returned to alcoholic obscurity.

All this could be explained although not condoned, if McCarthy's national following had been impressive. But the only impressive thing about him at the height of his infamy was that he seemed to scare senators. (The outside world observing this hateful fact, could not be blamed for wondering whether the whole of great America was cowering before an evil fear monger).

Senators he could scare. And he did scare poor little people who might lose their jobs because of his conscienceless changes... But to the responsible press he was always a scandal compounded with a bad joke.

## SOURCE 2

Extract from the Tydings Committee report. The Tydings Committee was set up in February 1950 to investigate McCarthy's accusations against the State Department.

... We have carefully and conscientiously viewed each and every one of the loyalty files relative to the individuals charged by Senator McCarthy. In no instance was any one of them now employed in the State Department found to be a 'card carrying Communist', a member of the Communist party or 'loyal to the Communist Party'. Furthermore in no instance have we found in our considered judgement that the decision to grant loyalty and security clearance has been erroneously or improperly made in the light of existing loyalty standards.

Otherwise stated, we do not find basis in any instance of reversing the judgement of the State Department officials charged with responsibility for employee loyalty, or concluding that they have not conscientiously discharged their duties ...

We are fully satisfied therefore on the basis of our study of the loyalty files, that the State Department has not knowingly retained in its employ individuals who have been disloyal.

 **Use the context**

Having completed the previous activity, read the following statements and work out how to use the context to support the following claims. Write a sentence justifying each of the claims.

- Source 1 is correct to argue that McCarthy was an even greater threat to President Eisenhower than he had been to President Truman because...
- Source 2 refuted the allegations of Senator McCarthy concerning Communist infiltration in the State Department because...

# Anti-Communism and the Cold War

REVISED

One reason for the credibility given to the findings of McCarthy and HUAC was the fear as a result of the Cold War. This was heightened by the genuine fear of Communist infiltration and nuclear attack developed during the Cold War.

## The Cold War context

There was a real fear of Communist attack from the USSR or China. Many Americans feared Western Europe would be taken over by Communists. President **Truman** had spoken of the need for **containment** to prevent Communism from spreading. Marshall Aid was designed to help European economies recover to prevent Communist takeovers. The USA had risked war over the **Berlin Airlift**, and had been involved in a full-scale war in Korea.

## Government actions to prevent Communist infiltration

The Government passed various measures to prevent Communist infiltration. All these added to the sense of a real fear:

- 1950 McCarran Internal Security Act forced all Communist organisations to register with the Attorney General and prevented any Communists from working in defence organisations
- 1954 Communist Control Act made it illegal to communicate any Communist ideas.

## The reality of the nuclear age

While the USA had a monopoly of nuclear weapons, it felt relatively secure. However, by the 1950s the USSR had them too. Both sides were entering into an arms race – the USA spent $40 to $50 billion on defence per year in the 1950s. Additionally, 90 per cent of its foreign aid went on military spending. The fear of nuclear attack was exacerbated by regular drills and simulations, which only reinforced the message for many that in the event of such an attack, most people would die and society would be destroyed.

This, of course, was inconsistent with the enthusiasm with which the military adopted nuclear testing. In one exercise 60,000 military personnel took part with no protective clothing to study the psychological effects of nuclear fallout. Similar tests took place near to inhabited areas in Nevada.

## Duck and cover

Until the 1960s the official line was that society could withstand nuclear attack. An 'Alert America' programme was developed to reassure people that simple civil defence measures would be adequate in the event of a nuclear attack. Pamphlets and films reinforced the message – including 'Duck and cover' aimed at children featuring a cartoon turtle called Bert.

## Spy scares

The fears of Communist infiltration and attack were exacerbated by a series of spy scares during the late 1940s and early 1950s, in which scientists and officials working on nuclear projects had passed secrets on to the Russians. The Soviets claimed they had at least 221 spies working in US government.

The fears were highlighted in a series of high-profile trials, notably that of Alger Hiss, a senior State Department official accused of promoting Russian interests over a period of time. However, it was the case of the Rosenbergs that received most notoriety.

### Ethel and Julius Rosenberg

The Rosenbergs were scientists accused of passing on nuclear secrets to the Russians. Such was the fear that they were executed in 1953, despite the paucity of evidence against them. These executions were opposed by many people and to some extent calmed the paranoia which had gripped much of the USA.

**Develop the detail**

Below are a sample exam question and a paragraph written in answer to this question. The paragraph contains a limited amount of detail. Annotate the paragraph to add additional detail to the answer.

How far was the Cold War responsible for the second Red Scare of the early 1950s?

The Cold War was in a large way responsible for the second Red Scare of the early 1950s. There was a real fear of Communist attack from the USSR or China. Many Americans feared Europe would be taken over by Communists. President Truman had spoken of Containment to prevent Communism from spreading. There were various crises in the late 1940s, which could have led to war between the superpowers, and in the early 1950s the USA became involved in the Korean War. In the 1950s too, the threat grew worse because the USSR also gained nuclear weapons. Both sides spent much of their budgets on defence. The tension and hostilities resulting from the Cold War were therefore largely responsible for the second Red Scare of the early 1950s.

 **You're the examiner**                                                                 **a**

Below are a sample exam question and a paragraph written in answer to this question. Read the paragraph and the mark scheme provided on page 102. Decide which level you would award the paragraph. Write the level below, along with a justification for your choice.

How accurate is it to say that, during the years 1945–55 the second Red Scare resulted from real fears of Communist infiltration in the USA?

During the period 1945 to 1955 there was a real fear of Communist infiltration in the USA, initially through the investigations of HUAC, into Communist infiltration into labour unions and government departments, notably the State Department.

The House Un-American Activities Committee had indeed been investigating Communist influences since 1945. Its reports and the publicity they occasioned led to fears of Communist infiltration, which fuelled the second Red Scare. There was a real fear of Communism in the late 1940s exacerbated by the development of nuclear weapons by the USSR in 1949, which put them on equal terms with the USA. The USA had faced external threats from the expansion of Communism in Europe through the development of Communist satellites in Eastern Europe and the ongoing question of the post-war settlement of Germany, which saw Berlin in particular as a flashpoint. However, the USA had a monopoly of nuclear weapons until 1949, which was a useful barrier to Communist aggression. Equality here made the Korean War far more dangerous in the sense of the possible results of escalation.

Reason for choosing this level and this mark:

_____

_____

# Cultural change: Hollywood and the Cold War

The post-war period saw many cultural changes, notably the rising influence of television, sponsored by relentless advertising. It was also a time when some stereotyping, for example, against members of different ethnic groups, was beginning to break down. However, this was a slow process.

## Hollywood and the Cold War

As Hollywood was investigated by HUAC many producers sought to demonstrate their patriotism by making movies in which the villains were Communists. Of course many of these were simply a variation on the traditional theme of cops and robbers. In *Big Jim McLain* (1952), for example, John Wayne plays a HUAC investigator who acts like a policeman in investigating the evil activities of Communists. Some films, however, had deeper messages. For example, *I Married a Communist* (1950) shows how a person's past could catch up with him, while *My Son John* (1952) presents the anguish of parents who suspect their son is a Communist spy. While many films alerted viewers to the Communist threat at home, others actually depicted events of the Cold War such as *The Big Lift* (1950), which dealt with the Berlin Airlift, and *Pork Chop Hill* (1959,) which was about the reality of fighting in the Korean War. As in earlier war films the new Cold War films sacrificed glamour and excitement for a more realistic portrayal as if to emphasise the Cold War was real.

## Science fiction

Many Cold War films used science fiction as an analogy: monsters were often robotic or homogenous like Communists; this is exemplified in *The War of the Worlds* (1953) in which the alien invaders lack any individuality.

## Religion

Films with biblical themes such as *Quo Vadis* (1951) and *The Robe* (1953) were also popular in the 1950s. Some argued that these reassured audiences that the USA maintained its religious beliefs, unlike godless Communists. The influential Christian evangelist Billy Graham claimed atheism was masterminded by Communists.

To some extent the Cold War simply served as a backdrop for thrillers whose villains were Communists rather than criminals. They did however tap into real fears of Communist infiltration.

## Decline in the popularity of films

However, the post-war period saw the popularity of films declining, despite lavish productions and the introduction of new techniques such as 3D to maintain their appeal. Cinema attendances declined from approximately 90 million in 1946 to 60 million by 1950 and around 46 million in 1955. It is worth noting that while the advent of television was the main reason for the decline in cinema-going during the 1950s, the decline predated this.

### Reasons for decline

- The movement to suburbs meant fewer people had ready access to cinemas.
- Hollywood itself came under attack for subversion (see page 80) and scandals involving stars such as drunkenness and sexual licence, which threatened traditional views of morality.

However, the most important reason was that cinema could not compete with television as people increasingly preferred to be entertained in the privacy of their own homes.

# Establish criteria

Below is a sample exam question, which requires you to make a judgement. The key term in the question has been underlined. Defining the meaning of the key term can help you establish criteria that you can use to make a judgement.

Read the question, define the key term and then set out two or three criteria based on the key term, which you can use to reach and justify a judgement.

How accurate is it to say that Cold War fears dominated Hollywood productions during the period 1945 to 1955?

Definition:

_____

_____

Criteria to judge the extent to which Cold War fears dominated Hollywood productions during the period 1945 to 1955.

- _____

- _____

- _____

- _____

# Reach a judgement

Having defined the key term and established a series of criteria, you should now make a judgement. Consider how far Cold War fears dominated Hollywood productions during the period 1945 to 1955 according to each criterion. Summarise your judgements below:

- Criterion 1:

_____

- Criterion 2:

_____

- Criterion 3:

_____

- Criterion 4:

_____

Finally, sum up your judgement. Based on the criteria, how accurate is it to say that Cold War fears dominated Hollywood productions during the period 1945 to 1955?

_____

_____

_____

Tip: remember you should weigh up evidence of films showing fears of Communism against other factors in the film industry such as its attempts to maintain audiences in your conclusion.

# Cultural change: The growing power of television and the origins of teenage culture

REVISED

During the 1950s television became a national phenomenon in terms of growth and popularity. The number of sets rose from 60,000 in 1947 to 37 million by 1955; in 1950, 3.9 million households had televisions and in 1955 30.7 million (some households had more than one), reflecting an 87 per cent increase in five years. A poll conducted by Paramount Film Studios found families with TVs decreased their cinema-going by 20 to 30 per cent. TV became the principal form of entertainment during the 1950s.

## TV stations

The number of TV stations increased from 98 in 1950 to 233 by 1954. They were all commercial concerns whose programmes were sponsored by advertisers in order to sell more of their products. For example, Colgate toothpaste sponsored the **NBC network** Comedy Hour from 1950 to 1955. Disney began a trend in tie-in merchandising with their *Davy Crockett* series. Indeed, Davy Crockett-style coonskin caps brought the company $300,000 worth of sales.

## Popular TV

Television mainly provided escapist entertainment for millions of viewers. It is estimated that half the population saw entertainer Mary Martin take to the air as Peter Pan in a 1955 spectacular. Nonetheless, it could also be very powerful. Journalist and broadcaster Edward R Murrow was concerned that if TV only provided entertainment it would become the **opiate of the people**. His hard-hitting documentary series *See It Now* helped expose Joseph McCarthy (see page 80). Current affairs programmes often had an important impact.

However, most viewers preferred popular TV. Situation comedies (sit-coms) such as *I Love Lucy* featuring comedy actress Lucille Ball attracted 50 million viewers. Ironically Lucille Ball may have played a dizzy blonde who created comic mayhem, but in reality she was a powerful entrepreneur who broke the stereotypical mould of passive females (see page 88) by being both performer and producer in the series. TV tended to promote family values, and was dominated by white, middle-class actors. *Leave it to Beaver* was typical of early 50s American television as the central character learned that his father was always right and the family was the strongest influence for good.

TV dramas included westerns and detective series, which promoted the American values that grit and determination could overcome all odds and good always prevailed.

## The origins of a teenage culture

In the early 1950s, most of the US population were young. Indeed, in 1950 41.6 per cent of the population was under 24. Many teenagers had jobs and surplus income. Therefore, a dedicated market developed to cater for their interests, producing teen fashions and music. Hollywood studios also produced films specifically aimed at a teenage market, such as *I Was a Teenage Werewolf* (1957).

## Rock and Roll

The mid-1950s saw performers, such as Elvis Presley and Jerry Lee Lewis, rise to national prominence. Their music, known as rock and roll, offered an exuberant beat, which facilitated wild dancing – and young people embraced it with enthusiasm. Many older people, however, tended to dislike it because of its sexual energy and sense of rebellion. Some white parents also feared the black American roots of rock and roll would lead their children into immorality, sexual licence and mixing with those of other ethnic origins.

However, for most teenagers any rebellion was a phase and most grew up to become just as conservative as their parents.

##  Write the question

The following sources relate to the growth and impact of TV. Read the guidance detailing what you need to know about the growth of TV during this period. Having done this, write an exam-style question using the sources.

How far could the historian make use of Sources 1 and 2 together to investigate...?

_____

_____

Explain your answer, using both sources, the information given about them and your own knowledge of the historical context.

Why is Source 1 valuable to the historian for an enquiry into...?

_____

_____

Explain your answer using the source, the information given about it and your own knowledge of the historical context. **AS**

## SOURCE 1

From *The Life and Times of the Thunderbolt Kid,* written in 2007. Bill Bryson is a popular writer; *The Life and Times of the Thunderbolt Kid* is his memoir of growing up during the 1950s. Here he is discussing the impact of TV in his household.

C.A. Swanson and Sons of Omaha came up with the perfect product in 1954: TV dinners... possibly the best made food ever produced, and I mean that as the sincerest of compliments. TV dinners gave you a whole meal on a compartmentalised aluminium tray... Then some innovative genius produced special folding trays that you could eat from while watching television and that was the last time any child indeed any male human being – sat at a dining table voluntarily.

Of course it wasn't TV as we know it now. For one thing commercials were often built right into the programmes which gave them an endearing and guileless charm. On Burns and Allen (a sitcom), my favourite programme, an announcer named Harry von Zell would show up halfway through and stroll up into George and Grace's kitchen and do a commercial for Carnation Evaporated Milk... while George and Grace obligingly waited till he was finished to continue that week's amusing story.

... Adverts dominated every aspect of production. Writers working on shows sponsored by Camel cigarettes were forbidden to show villains smoking cigarettes, to make any mention in any context of fires or arson or anything to do with smoke and flames, or to have anyone cough for any reason.

## SOURCE 2

Taken from *The Television Code of the National Association of Radio and Television Broadcasters,* effective from March 1954. This was a code of practice for TV producers.

Television is seen and heard in every type of American home. These homes include children and adults of all ages, embrace all races and all varieties of religious faith, and reach those of every educational background. It is the responsibility of television to bear constantly in mind that the audience is primarily a home audience, and consequently that television's relationship to the viewers is that between guest and host.

The revenues from advertising support the free, competitive American system of telecasting, and make available to the eyes and ears of the American people the finest programs of information, education, culture and entertainment. By law the television broadcaster is responsible for the programming of his station. He, however, is obligated to bring his positive responsibility for excellence and good taste in programming to bear upon all who have a hand in the production of programs, including networks, sponsors, producers of film and of live programs, advertising agencies, and talent agencies.

# The stereotyping of women and ethnic minorities

REVISED

## Stereotyping

TV reflected white middle-class values. It promoted a message of what the ideal family should be like. In particular, it depicted women as homemakers. Black people were rarely seen on TV, except as servants, criminals, or figures of fun. Indeed, the only show in the 1950s with a black American as the central character was *Beulah*, about a domestic servant.

## Women

Women were generally depicted in the media as wives and mothers. Many women's magazines concentrated on articles about homecare, fashion and how to keep your husband happy. Advertising was dominated by images of contented housewives and loving mothers who were delighted to receive the latest household appliance as a birthday or Christmas present. One important influence in keeping women at home was Dr Spock, whose childcare manuals, emphasising the need for a mother's presence, sold in their millions. Feminist Betty Friedan found in 1957 that 85 percent of graduates from the all-female Smith College were homemakers without paid full-time employment

The overwhelming media image of women was of middle-class white housewives. Indeed, less affluent or women from ethnic minority backgrounds barely featured in the US media, except as domestic servants.

## Political and professional involvement

The emphasis on women as homemakers was reflected in their under-representation in politics and the professions. In 1953 there were still only ten women in the House of Representatives and three female Senators. Meanwhile, by 1955 only around six per cent of management positions were held by women. Indeed, only one-third of women in college actually graduated; most left early, often to marry.

Not all women were content with this state of affairs. Many women's magazines produced articles reflecting their frustrations at the lack of professional opportunities.

## Changing attitudes

Attitudes were slowly changing, however. Hollywood in particular showed strong female characters played by assertive actresses, such as Joan Crawford, Bette Davis and Katharine Hepburn. Some more radical magazines such as *Redbook* also began publishing articles on how many women felt dissatisfied and trapped.

## The stereotyping of black Americans

Black Americans, if featured in the media at all, were often shown as lazy, or devious figures of fun. They rarely appeared, unless the script specifically demanded such characters. It was rare, for example, to show black American actors without comment on their skin colour. Some black Americans however, were breaking down the stereotype. The NAACP, for example, arranged a boycott of Blatz beer, which sponsored the *Amos 'n' Andy Show*, a TV show developed from the radio series (see page 24), which ridiculed blacks. Mainly, however, in TV and films, black Americans were noticeable by their absence.

The only area where black Americans did have widespread respect remained in music. It was during the 1950s that jazz and blues music developed into rock and roll.

## Native Americans

One area where stereotypes were breaking down was in the depiction of Native Americans, previously seen as vicious savages in countless Western films. They were shown in a more sympathetic light in films such as *Broken Arrow* (1951) and in *Apache* (1954) where emphasis was placed on the loss of their land and destruction of their culture and white villains were shown as exploiting them.

## Add the context

Below is a sample A Level exam question with the accompanying sources. Having read the question and the sources, complete the following activity.

> How far could the historian make use of Sources 1 and 2 together to investigate the issue of stereotyping of black Americans in the media in the period 1945 to 1955?

First, look for aspects of the source that offer evidence of the ways in which black Americans were stereotyped. Underline the key phrases and write a brief description of the context of how black Americans were treated at the time in the margin next to the source (you could find more information about this from page 90). Draw an arrow from the key phrase to the context. Try to find three key phrases in each source.

Tip: look at the information above the source – you should contextualise this too. Pay particular attention to the purpose for which the sources were produced.

## SOURCE 1

Extract from a script for the *Amos 'n' Andy Show* (from the early 1950s). This was a long-running comedy on radio and TV that stereotyped black Americans as lazy and unintelligent.

AMOS: If you don't give me my money back, I'm going to punch you in each eye! Then I'm going to punch you in the mouth! Then I'm going to take a stick and crack your head! In other words, I'm going to open everything that's closed, and close everything that's open! ...

KINGFISH: You know of course that there's a shortage of women!

ANDY: I'll say, the one I took out last night only come up to my belt buckle!

SAPPHIRE: It's about time you met some decent people instead of that horrible uncouth group that you associate with!

KINGFISH: Well I've done met all the accomplished people I want to know.

SAPPHIRE: Like Andrew Brown for instance.

KINGFISH: Yeah! Like Andrew Brown!

SAPPHIRE: Well what may I ask has he ever accomplished?

KINGFISH: Well he uh... just yesterday, he had a run of thirteen balls in the five pocket without once leaning on the pool table!

SAPPHIRE: That's just what I'm talking about. Andrew hanging over a pool table! You'll never find him in a public library!

KINGFISH: No, they ain't got no pool table in there!

## SOURCE 2

From Cecil Roberts, *And So To America*, written in 1947. Roberts was a British journalist who was writing mainly for a British audience about his visit to the USA.

It would be wrong to leave an impression that the Negro is everywhere an oppressed miserable victim of the white man. Many of them enjoy life, however lowly their estate. I would call them a happy race. They sing, they laugh, they dance and they doze in a manner that rebukes the pushful, over-organised white folk... I had an opportunity of observing and listening to them. They told some strange stories, consciously indulging in exaggeration; indeed many of them were poets at heart. They chuckled over their own absurdities. They were workers on the levee that kept the unruly Mississippi [river] on its course, cotton pickers, and farm workers, men of stringy physique and patient endurance, but all happy-go-lucky with the gambling instinct strong in them... I never received any inkling that they felt racially inferior, and never heard them make any complaint about their lot although I am certain they were conscious of exploitation.

The Negro is the American headache.

# The changing status of minorities

The status of ethnic minorities began slowly to improve during the post-war period, although it was an uneven process and real changes would have to wait for later periods.

## Native Americans

Many Native Americans had no desire to return to the reservations and questioned their economic viability. This led to a change in government policy back to assimilation.

## Termination

President Eisenhower favoured a policy of termination by which the reservation system would be ended and Native Americans could live and work as ordinary Americans. In 1953 it was announced that the reservations should be broken up and the lands sold off. However, this policy needed the consent of the different Native American tribes and was very unpopular. As a result, progress was very slow. By 1960 only three per cent of reservation land had been sold and only 13,000 Native Americans had moved permanently. In the 1960s, the policy of termination was abandoned.

## Hispanic Americans

There were plentiful employment opportunities in the fruit farms of California for Hispanic Americans. The bracero program invited temporary labour from Latin America to augment US labour. Between 1950 and 1954 possibly as many as 200,000 Hispanic people entered the USA under the scheme each year; many more crossed illegally. The work remained poorly paid and working conditions hard.

Although many workers continued to face discrimination, the 1950s nevertheless saw a resurgence in interest among Americans in Latin American culture, from popular music to architecture.

## Black Americans

The post-war period saw real legal measures to improve the lives of black Americans.

Presidents Truman and Eisenhower were reluctant to commit themselves to civil rights, although both saw that change must come and set precedents for the future.

## The growth of the National Association for the Advancement of Colored People (NAACP)

The NAACP was founded in 1909 to promote the cause of racial equality both through direct action such as protest and through the law courts. It had focused in more recent years on political rights and education and was energised in the 1950s by successes in cases relating to the provision of higher education for black Americans.

## The desegregation of the armed forces

In July 1948 Executive Order 9981 desegregated the armed forces and guaranteed fair employment opportunities in the civil service. Despite fears among the senior personnel, desegregation went well and soldiers fought together irrespective of ethnic origin during the Korean War. Even training camps in the South managed to integrate successfully. This helped give black Americans hope for the future.

Eisenhower continued this process with Executive Orders, which desegregated government-run shipyards and veterans' hospitals, and also tried to desegregate schools in Washington, particularly after the landmark Brown v. Topeka ruling in 1954.

## The Brown case 1954 (Brown v. Topeka)

Brown v. Topeka concerned equal education in schools. The NAACP brought a case to defend the rights of Linda Brown, a seven-year-old black girl in Topeka, Kansas. Brown could not attend her nearest school because of racial segregation. On 17 May 1954 the Supreme Court ruled that segregation had no place in education.

However, the ruling did not lead to desegregation. The Supreme Court imposed no sanctions and said it was the responsibility of local authorities to implement it. Most Southern states ignored the ruling – 240,000 black children in the South remained in segregated schools. President Eisenhower was ambivalent about it – privately he was furious about the Supreme Court ruling, because he believed that it reflected militant demands, and would cause a **white backlash**, which would make the situation in the South worse.

**Qualify your judgement**

Below is a sample A Level exam question with the accompanying sources. Having read the question and the sources, complete the following activity.

How far could the historian make use of Sources 1 and 2 together to investigate the impact of the Supreme Court Brown v. Topeka ruling of 1954 on racial integration?

Below are three judgements about the value of Source 1 to a historian investigating the impact of the Brown v. Topeka case. Circle the judgement that best described the value of the source, and explain why it is the best.

1 Source 1 is partially valuable to a historian investigating the impact of Brown v. Topeka because it shows the fears about racial mixing which could arrive from desegregating schools. Cooke does not seem hopeful. However, it lacks specific examples so it is the view of one person without hard evidence in support.

2 Source 1 is unreliable to a historian because Cooke is a British journalist so unlikely to understand the impact of events in the USA.

3 Source 1 is valuable to a historian investigating the impact of Brown v. Topeka because it shows us the pessimistic views of a British journalist. He also suggests it wouldn't make much difference because 31 states where schools are integrated still have laws banning mixed marriages. President Eisenhower once said that you couldn't change people's hearts through legislation.

The best judgement about the value of Source 1 is _____ because _____.

Now apply what you have learned by writing a judgement about the value of Source 2 for a historian investigating the impact of the Brown v. Topeka ruling.

_____

_____

## SOURCE 1

From *'The Court and the Negro', by Alistair Cooke,* 20 August 1954. Cooke was a British journalist resident in the USA who read a weekly 'Letter from America' on BBC radio. Here he is discussing the impact of the Brown v. Topeka case.

... it seems to me, at least, frivolous and superficial not to face the fact that after a generation or so of mixed schooling, social barriers will tumble, young people will pick their friends for themselves, they will fall in love, as they do everywhere, with the girls and boys around them.

This is a consummation which is at present ignored. The traditions of American life are strong enough, so far, to make intermarriage prohibitive in the thirty-one states where white and coloured go to the same schools. Oddly, it is in the south where the races are separated in school and church and in theatres, that the Negro is woven deep in the texture of society. And it is in the south where the test will come of whether the white man can live and work with the black man as a social and political equal which has at least relaxed the tensions of three hundred years. In the exhilaration of the Supreme Court's trumpet call, we should not, I think, expect too much of whites now, or later.

## SOURCE 2

From Brown v. Board of Education of Topeka Ruling by the Supreme Court, 14 May 1954.

To separate them [black Americans] from others of similar age and qualifications solely because of their race generates a feeling of inferiority as to their status in the community that may affect their hearts and minds in a way unlikely ever to be undone. The effect of this separation on their educational opportunities was well stated by a finding in the Kansas case by a court which nevertheless felt compelled to rule against the Negro plaintiffs:

"Segregation of white and colored children in public schools has a detrimental effect upon the colored children. The impact is greater when it has the sanction of the law, for the policy of separating the races is usually interpreted as denoting the inferiority of the negro group. A sense of inferiority affects the motivation of a child to learn. Segregation with the sanction of law, therefore, has a tendency to [retard] the educational and mental development of negro children and to deprive them of some of the benefits they would receive in a racial[ly] integrated school system."

# The extent of change by 1955

In the post-war period America continued to be a white-dominated society. However, there were some indicators that the status of black people was changing.

## Entertainment

Black music such as jazz and blues had long been popular with black and white audiences. While many performers such as Louis Armstrong enjoyed widespread popularity, some such as Harry Belafonte began to drive a shift in films too. He starred, for example, in *Islands in the Sun* (1956), which showed inter-racial romance. Hollywood traditionally had used black performers as domestic servants or figures of fun, but Belafonte starred in one of the first films to show a romance between a black man and a white woman. This was a radical depiction of equality that challenged white prejudices about the relationship between black people and white people.

While there had been earlier attempts such as in *Pinky* (1949) to show black Americans in a positive light, many producers were reluctant to promote racial equality because of its association with Communism, and films with strong black characters and casts did remain in the minority.

The issue was exacerbated by the fact that Hollywood was under threat from television, and people in the South remained the most loyal cinemagoers – the very audiences who would least tolerate movies with strong black American leads.

## Sport

The USA had accepted black sporting heroes if they really excelled. As such, they tended to be 'one-offs'. Black tennis player Anthea Gibson, for example, won accolades in the 1950s but had no successors until the rise of Arthur Ashe in the 1960s.

Both American football and baseball were integrated in 1946 by the introduction of players of sublime talent, Bill Willis and Jackie Robinson respectively, but their success did not lead to large numbers of black American professionals in these sports. Indeed, in baseball some teams had unwritten quotas of four non-white players. Integration may have begun but it was slow.

It must be said too that whites were more prepared to accept black American athletes as this reinforced the idea that they may be physically strong but white people were still intellectually superior.

## White backlash

While authorities, particularly in the South, had hoped to ignore the Brown v. Topeka ruling (see page 90), local courts increasingly supported it.

White racist anger at the Brown case led to an increase in white racist violence. The Ku Klux Klan (see page 16) saw a resurgence of membership and some horrific murders took place – for example, in August 1955 of schoolboy Emmet Till, who had been accused of showing disrespect to a white shop assistant.

### Citizens' Councils

Citizens' Councils were formed of influential people in a community who might, for example, boycott the businesses of those who supported desegregation. By 1956 they claimed 500,000 members.

By 1955 the battle for equal rights in the USA had a long way to go.

# Establish criteria

Below is a sample exam question which requires you to make a judgement. The key term in the question has been underlined. Defining the meaning of the key term can help you establish criteria that you can use to make a judgement.

Read the question, define the key term and then set out two or three criteria based on the key term, which you can use to reach and justify a judgement.

'In the period 1945–55 there was a <u>significant improvement in the status of</u> black Americans.' How far do you agree with this statement?

Definition:

_____

_____

Criteria to judge the extent to which the battle for equal rights had won significant victories by 1955:

- _____

- _____

- _____

- _____

# Reach a judgement

Having defined the key term and established a series of criteria, you should now make a judgement. Consider how far significant victories in the battles for equal rights had been won by 1955 according to each criterion. Summarise your judgements below:

- Criterion 1:

_____

- Criterion 2:

_____

- Criterion 3:

_____

- Criterion 4:

_____

Finally, sum up your judgement. Based on the criteria, how accurate is it to say that significant victories had been won in the battle for equal rights by 1955?

_____

_____

_____

Tip: remember you should weigh up evidence of modernisation against evidence of failure in your conclusion.

# Exam focus

Below are a sample A Level exam style question and a model answer. Read the answer and the comments around it.

'There was little change in the role and status of women during the period 1920 to 1955.' How far do you agree with this statement?

During the period 1920 to 1955 the role and status of women appeared to change comparatively little. It was affected by traditional attitudes, which saw women as primarily concerned with domestic issues and childcare, and the impact of economic Depression, which reduced women's already limited career prospects. However, their position did fluctuate at different periods with the war from 1941 to 1945, in particular the emergence of more opportunities, which many were subsequently reluctant to relinquish. Much depends too on which groups of women one is discussing. There were usually more opportunities for single younger women, although surveys throughout the period 1920 to 1955 found that the goal for many was marriage, and career was subsidiary to this.

**Clear question focus, showing understanding of range of question.**

Women had very limited career and political opportunities during the 1920s. Although the 19th Amendment of 1920 gave them the right to vote, it made little difference to their everyday lives. While on the surface they could participate in politics and hold political office equally with men, in practice they enjoyed very limited opportunities in politics. Political representation remained sparse. While only 145 women held seats on the various state legislatures in 1928, there were only two delegates in the 435-strong House of Representatives and no female senators. By 1953 the number had risen to 12 and three respectively.

**Good use of knowledge in support.**

Throughout the period, except during the war years, the vast majority of working women remained in relatively low-paid employment such as shop work or clerical, or in menial jobs such as domestic service – where in the 1920s 700,000, many of them black Americans, found employment. Even when women did the same jobs as men they received less pay. The economic status of women therefore changed little over the period as a whole.

Moreover, where women enjoyed an enhanced role in the public sphere as opposed to the home, the development was at best temporary. In the 1920s, for example, it seemed that the status of young women was improving. Much was made of the 'flappers' – young single women in employment and adopting hedonistic lifestyles. Evidence suggests, however, that flappers were very much a product of the cities and most saw it as a phase before marriage and domesticity. Similarly, in wartime, the media promotion of role models such as Rosie the Riveter could not negate that most saw the employment of young women in hitherto male-associated roles as temporary expedients. In the 1950s it was assumed all young women sought marriage and domesticity and the media was very much geared to this view.

**Relative significance of criteria, i.e. independence of young single women considered.**

The fact that women, like men, are individuals and do not normally act as a group as a whole, served to negate any real change in their role and status as they rarely campaigned for improvements as a sex. While women faced common issues they did not of course vote as a homogenous group and had as many different views on issues as men. Indeed, while this point became more significant as active feminism developed, it was always evident. During the 1920s, for example, many women were increasingly concerned with issues such as birth control. Other Christian women, however, saw this as immoral. One of the few measures aimed at women was the 1921 Sheppard–Towner Act, which gave states federal aid to develop healthcare for pregnant women. However, many feminists believed this simply reinforced the role of women as child-bearers and detracted from the need for birth control. Women were rarely as able to present a united front as men. Feminists in the 1920s also criticised

**Emphasises the important point that women are not a homogenous group.**

legislation aimed to protect women in the workplace, such as the banning of nightshift work for women. In practice, this tended to mean those affected lost their jobs, thus making them even more dependent on men. It also highlighted a significant split between those women who felt protection in law for women was necessary and those who believed in equal treatment. This further illustrates the complexity of attitudes on women's issues to reinforce the point that a united front is often impossible to achieve and means they rarely if ever focus as a whole group on a particular issue, which would improve their role and status.

Using specific examples to illustrate a general point.

The Depression and New Deal years saw little change for women in terms of role and status. The onset of the Depression saw women particularly badly affected as they were often the first to lose their jobs, while half the 48 states actually banned the employment of married women. The New Deal did comparatively little to help women. While there were high-profile female appointments, such as Frances Perkins as Secretary of Labor, and Eleanor Roosevelt who was a very active First Lady with a particular interest in gender issues, most found measures worked against them – the Economy Act of 1933, for example, forbade members of the same family from working for federal government and 75 per cent of those who subsequently lost their jobs were women. In this sense, if anything, their role and status diminished during the Depression and New Deal years.

Much covered here – possibly could be more developed.

The war years did, however, see some improvement in their role and status. The onset of war saw a resurgence of female labour, which was, of course, necessary as men joined the armed forces. Nevertheless, women received unequal pay, and Labour unions often emphasised their employment was temporary until hostilities ended. The numbers of women as a percentage of the workforce in manufacturing industry rose from 22 to 32 per cent between 1941 and 1944 and much was made of this for propaganda purposes. It also gave women more confidence as they both worked and supported families without their partners who were serving in the military. Many overcame huge problems having to juggle childcare with long hours of employment. There was in particular a shortage of food to buy and a shortage of housing in urban areas. Although they overcame these to considerable media acclaim, there was nevertheless an expectation that they would return to domesticity when the war was over. The enhanced role and status in wartime resulted therefore from what was seen as a temporary expedient and would itself not be permanent.

Emphasis on atypicality of wartime period.

This was reinforced in the post-war period where women generally were depicted in the media as wives and mothers. One significant influence was Dr Spock, whose million-selling childcare manuals emphasised the need for a mother's presence and love. Many periodicals concentrated on articles about homecare, fashion and how to keep husbands happy. Advertising was dominated by images of contented housewives and loving mothers who were delighted to receive the latest household appliance as a birthday or Christmas present. Attitudes were slowly changing, however. Hollywood in particular showed strong female characters played by assertive actresses, such as Joan Crawford, Bette Davis and Katharine Hepburn. Some periodicals such as *Redbook* were beginning to publish articles on how many women felt dis-satisfied and trapped. The feminist Betty Frieden was undertaking work on women's frustrations.

One can see therefore that while there were peaks and troughs of opportunity, the overwhelming view of the role and status of women during the period 1920 to 1955 was one of domesticity and childcare. While wartime did bring real opportunities, it also saw real challenges, and was seen moreover as an aberration. The 1950s saw a return very much to limited opportunities and aspirations – although female disaffection was given more of a voice. The role of women as shown in the media in 1955 was very similar to that depicted in 1920 – and that in itself might be a telling comment on how far their role and status had improved.

Conclusion reaches reasoned judgement based on what has been argued. The essay has maintained a tight focus.

This is an excellent essay with sustained analysis of key features such as political, economic and social status, with sufficient knowledge deployed to answer the key aspects of the question. The overall judgement is based in valid criteria. The structure is sound, with precise communication. It isn't perfect – the economic issues are rather hurried. Nevertheless, this would be marked at high Level 5.

---

**What makes a good answer?**

You have now considered four high-level essays. Use these essays (see pages 26, 48, 72 and 94) to make a bullet-pointed list of the characteristics of a top-level essay. Use this list when planning and writing your own practice exam essays.

---

## AS Level questions

How far do you agree that conditions for black Americans improved during the period 1945–55?

How accurate is it to say that the USA was involved in a Communist witch-hunt during the years 1945–55?

# Glossary

**Acreage**   Amount of land.

**Allotment**   Where pieces of land are made over by the Government to Native Americans.

**Alphabet agencies**   Term given to the agencies set up by the New Deal to address issues, so-called because they were known by their initials.

**Anarchism**   A political creed which does not believe in organised government.

**Anti-Semitic**   Anti-Jewish behaviour.

**Appropriation**   Money allocated by government bodies for a specific purpose.

**Assimilation**   The idea that Native Americans should adopt American lifestyles and values. Their traditional lifestyles would disappear.

**'back to the blanket'**   Return to Native American ways.

**Belligerents**   Countries at war.

**Berlin Airlift**   Supplies by air to West Berlin which was faced with a Blockade organised by the USSR to try to force it to accept Communism. The USA and Britain largely organised the airlift.

**Big three**   USA, USSR, UK; the three major allies during the Second World War.

**Bonus Army**   Term given to the groups who went to Washington in 1932 to demand their war pensions be paid early.

**Bracero program**   A programme of recruitment of labour from Latin America which ran from 1942 to 1964.

**Bull market**   Stock market where there is lots of confidence and lots of buying and selling.

**Bureau of Indian Affairs**   A federal government agency responsible for the administration and management of Native American land.

**Cold War**   From c1946 to c1987, the USA and the Soviet Union were antagonists in a war that was 'cold' in that neither directly attacked the other. Their enmity was caused by opposing ideologies. The USA believed in a multi-party state with a capitalist economy, while the Communist USSR favoured a single-party state and a state-controlled economy.

**Communism**   A political philosophy that favours a state-controlled economy and reward according to the value of one's input into the economy and society.

**Congress**   The Legislative body of the USA, comprising the House of Representatives, representing all citizens and the Senate representing the States. It can both initiate legislation, and discuss that introduced by the president.

**Consumerism**   Obsession with the acquisition of material goods.

**Containment**   United States foreign policy introduced at the start of the Cold War, aimed at stopping the spread of Communism and keeping it 'contained' and isolated within its current borders.

**Democrats**   The political party, or supporters of that party, which supports more government intervention and traditionally appeals to a wider cross-section of society than the Republicans.

**Farm Security Administration**   Alphabet agency originally set up as the Resettlement Administration in 1935 to help alleviate rural poverty.

**FBI**   Federal Bureau of Investigation, the internal crime-fighting and security organisation within the USA.

**Federal Reserve**   The organisation of banking in the USA where the major banks, formed into the Federal Reserve Board, were largely responsible for overseeing the banking system.

**Financial surplus**   Where the government income exceeds its spending.

**'fireside chats'**   Roosevelt's radio addresses to the electorate. Such was his warmth and charisma that it felt like he was speaking to people in their living rooms; hence the term 'fireside chats'.

**Fiscal conservative**   Someone who holds a political position that calls for lower levels of public spending, lower taxes and lower government debt.

**'flappers'**   Name given to young women who concentrated on having a good time, dancing, listening to music, watching films and so on.

**'furlough babies'**   Babies conceived a during furlough, a period of leave from the military.

**'ghettoes'**   Poor areas of cities where people of a particular ethnic group were concentrated.

**Government securities** Bonds and securities issued by the Government for sale to raise revenue.

**Great Depression** Term given to the massive economic downturn between 1929 and the mid-1930s.

**Gross Domestic Product (GDP)** The total value of goods produced and services provided in a country annually.

**Gross National Product (GNP)** The total value of goods and services produced in a country.

**'hoboes'** Itinerant workers who wandered around the USA in search of employment.

**Hoovervilles** Shanty towns built by homeless people during the Depression; they were named after Herbert Hoover, president during the onset of the Depression.

**House of Representatives** One of the two houses of Congress, representing citizens.

**House un-American Activities Committee (HUAC)** An investigative committee of the US House of Representatives, originally created in 1938 to uncover Nazi sympathisers but later expanded to investigate possible Communist Party infiltration.

**Insider dealing** Unfair practices in the Stock market – for example, brokers getting together to bring the value of particular stocks up or down.

**Korean War** War 1950–53 to prevent the spread of Communism to the Asian country of South Korea; the vast majority of the forces involved were from the USA.

**Laissez-faire** An approach where the Government deliberately avoids getting involved in economic planning, thus allowing free trade to operate.

**Management science** The application of technological and scientific ideas to running a company successfully – such as time and motion where the amount of time it should take to complete a process in manufacturing is timed and subsequently monitored. The aim is to use scientifically proven methods to run the company.

**Marshall Aid** Massive US aid to help Europe recover economically after the Second World War, specifically aimed to prevent the spread of Communism among Western European countries

**Mass production** Making large numbers of the same item using machinery and moving assembly lines.

**Mid-term Congressional Elections** Elections that take place every two years, halfway through the president's four-year term of office, usually a good indicator of the popularity of the president.

**Military-Industrial Complex** Term given to the relationship between the US military and the industrialists who supply it with materiel.

**National Association for the Advancement of Colored People (NAACP)** An organisation seeking to improve the lives of black Americans, often through the law courts.

**National infrastructure** The provision of public facilities, such as roads and hospitals, which allow the country to function efficiently.

**Nationalisation of public utilities** Where the state takes over the running of services such as electricity.

**NBC network** One of the national TV networks in the USA.

**'New Deal'** Name given to Roosevelt's programme to end the Depression and reform the US economy.

**'New immigrants'** Term referring to the waves of immigration largely from southern and eastern Europe in the late nineteenth and early twentieth centuries.

**Open market operations** Buying and selling government securities on the open market to control the money supply

**'opiate of the people'** Comment on television by broadcast journalist Edward R Murrow in despair at television's passive audience and poor programmes at the time.

**Per capita income** Income per head of the population.

**Prefabricated** Buildings such as houses coming in parts to be reassembled on site.

**President** The head of state and executive. The president is elected every four years.

US presidents 1921–61

| Years | President | Party |
|---|---|---|
| 1921–23 | Warren Harding (died 1923) | Republican |
| 1923–29 | Calvin Coolidge | Republican |
| 1929–33 | Herbert Hoover | Republican |
| 1933–45 | Franklin Delano Roosevelt (died 1945) | Democrat |
| 1945–53 | Harry S Truman | Democrat |
| 1953–61 | Dwight D Eisenhower | Republican |

**Prohibition** The banning of the manufacture, transportation and sale of alcohol for consumption.

**Protection**   Where a government limits imports or promotes exports by putting up barriers to trade.

**Pump-priming**   Expression used to suggest government spending would lead to economic growth.

**Recession**   A downturn in the economy.

**'Red Scare'**   Attack by the authorities who feared a Communist revolution, on people suspected of left-wing sympathies.

**Republican**   One of the two main political parties: they tend to favour wealth, business and a limited government role in the economy, supporting ideas such as *laissez-faire*.

**Reservation**   An area allocated for a specific group of Native Americans to live.

**Robin Hood**   Legendary English outlaw who stole from the rich to redistribute wealth to the poor

**Rugged Individualism**   Belief in people solving their own problems and not relying on the Government for help.

**Run on the bank**   Where savers lose confidence in their bank and rush to withdraw their deposits before it collapses.

**Segregated units**   Military units specifically for black Americans.

**Senate**   The house in Congress representing the states: each state, irrespective of size sent two Senators. During the period covered in this book there were 48 states.

**Separatism**   Different ethnic groups living apart from each other.

**Shanty towns**   Unplanned settlements on the edge of towns, often made of improvised materials, called during the Depression 'Hoovervilles'; an ironic reference to President Hoover's inability to deal effectively with the Depression.

**Sharecroppers**   Farmers who rented land and were paid by the landowners a percentage of what they produced.

**Shopping malls**   Large shopping precincts.

**Speculation**   Investment in stocks and property in the hope of gain but with the risk of loss.

**State Department**   Government department responsible for foreign affairs.

**State legislatures**   Law making bodies for the individual states.

**Subsistence**   Having just enough income to live on.

**Syndicated**   Where a newspaper or magazine column is sold to numerous publications.

**Synthetic fibres**   Textiles made from man-made resources as opposed, for example, to wool or cotton.

**Tariffs**   Import and export duties.

**Time and Motion techniques**   Management science techniques to time different stages and processes in production and set output targets accordingly.

**Tribal corporations**   Organisations to run tribal affairs on the reservations.

**Veterans' Association**   Organisation to manage the affairs of ex-servicemen.

**'Victory gardens'**   Gardens planted with fruit and vegetables in private residences and public parks to reduce pressure on the public food supply brought on by the war effort.

**Voluntarism**   The notion that business and state government should solve the Depression through their own voluntary efforts.

**Wall Street Stock Exchange**   The main Stock Exchange in the USA, based on Wall Street, New York City.

**War bonds**   Debt securities issued by the Government for the purpose of financing military operations during times of war.

**Wards**   A division of a city or town for administrative and representative purposes, especially during elections.

**War debts**   Debts accrued during the Great War, where the USA loaned the Allied powers the means to fight the war.

**War materiel**   Material needed for war.

**War pensions**   Pensions to be paid to war veterans at a specific time in the future, normally when most recipients would be of retirement age.

**White backlash**   Term referring to white reaction to what they perceive as too much immigration or integration with other ethnic groups.

**White goods**   Household appliances such as washing machines and refrigerators.

**White tourism**   Term referring to white people who visited black areas such as Harlem; they were accused of patronising attitudes, for example, regarding the inhabitants as animals to observe in a zoo.

**'Yellow Dog' clauses**   Where as part of their terms of employment employees had to agree not to join a labour union.

**'Zoot suits'**   Fashion trend favoured by Hispanic Americans during the 1940s, featuring long jackets, trousers baggy at the top and tight at the bottom, chains.

# Key figures

**Al Capone (1899–1947)** Capone was a gangster who made a fortune out of illegal activities in Chicago during the period of Prohibition. He became known for the ruthlessness and efficiency with which he controlled his operations. He seemed above the law largely because people were terrified to testify against him but was eventually jailed for income tax evasion in 1932.

**Calvin Coolidge (1872–1933)** Coolidge was a Republican politician who became president on the death of Warren Harding in 1923. He was associated with *laissez-faire* policies and the prosperity of the 1920s, but left office before the Wall Street Crash. He believed very much that a good government should do as little as possible and the economy was best left to business interests to run.

**Dwight D Eisenhower (1890–1969)** A career soldier who became Supreme Allied commander in Europe during the Second World War, masterminding the invasion of Northern Europe in 1945. He became Republican president in 1953, and presided over 1950s prosperity and the developing 'arms race'. Eisenhower retained great popularity, although he was a conservative who was reluctant to move on issues such as civil rights.

**Henry Ford (1863–1947)** Ford set up his company manufacturing motor vehicles in 1903 and pioneered techniques of mass production, which significantly reduced the cost of his cars. His economic success diminished as rivals such as General Motors emerged offering more choice and more advanced technology in their vehicles. Ford increasingly adopted right-wing political views before his death.

**Herbert Hoover (1874–1964)** Former mining engineer and millionaire businessman who served as Secretary of Commerce during the 1920s and became Republican president in 1929. His administration is dominated by his efforts to end the Depression but after his electoral defeat in 1932 he became a widely respected elder statesman.

**Huey Long (1893–1935)** Popular politician from Louisiana who adopted the 'Share Our Wealth' programme. He was considered a viable rival to Roosevelt for the 1936 Democratic nomination for president before being assassinated.

**Andrew Mellon (1855–1937)** Mellon was a wealthy banker and businessman who was appointed Secretary to the Treasury in March 1921. He was associated with *laissez-faire* policies, including prudence in government activity and spending, and believed the economy was best left to private enterprise. Mellon lost much credibility at the onset of the Depression. He resigned from the Treasury position in February 1932 and was appointed Ambassador to the UK for the remainder of president Hoover's administration.

**A Mitchell Palmer (1872–1936)** A Mitchell Palmer was a Democratic politician from Pennsylvania who was appointed Attorney General in March 1919. He is particularly associated with the Red Scare which he used as a springboard for his own presidential ambitions. However he lost credibility after his warnings of widespread insurrection in May 1920 failed to materialise. He retired from public office in 1921 but remained an influential figure in the Democratic Party.

**Eleanor Roosevelt (1884–1962)** She was very active as First Lady, promoting in particular gender and issues of race. Eleanor often reported directly to her husband about how well New Deal initiatives were working. She was also a high-profile journalist who encouraged people to contact her with their concerns. She expanded the role of First Lady into a more active, political role.

**Franklin Delano Roosevelt (1882–1945)** Former Secretary of the Navy and Governor of New York who became president in 1932 at the height of the Depression. In 1924 he contracted polio. His New Deal did much to transform the USA but enjoyed only limited economic success. Roosevelt remained president throughout the Second World War and died in office in April 1945.

**George Herman 'Babe' Ruth Junior (1895–1948)** Babe Ruth was a supremely talented baseball player who both helped to make the sport extremely popular and changed the image and livelihood of sporting heroes, growing wealthy as much through sponsorship as actual playing. Babe Ruth helped create the idea of sporting celebrity, although he dissipated much of his own wealth.

**Harry S Truman (1884–1972)** Democratic Senator from Missouri, and Vice President from January 1945 who unexpectedly became president on the death of Roosevelt in April. Truman made the decision to drop atomic bombs on Japan. He subsequently presided over post-war prosperity and the development of the Cold War.

# Timeline

| | | |
|---|---|---|
| 1919 | Eighteenth Amendment – introduction of Prohibition | |
| 1920 | Nineteenth Amendment – gave women the vote | |
| | Palmer Raids | |
| 1921 | Presidency of Warren Harding | |
| | Sheppard–Towner Act | |
| 1923 | Ku Klux Klan claimed 5,000,000 members | |
| | Death of President Harding: the presidency of Calvin Coolidge | |
| 1924 | Johnson–Reed Immigration Act | |
| 1926 | End of the Florida Land Boom | |
| 1927 | Execution of Saccho and Vanzetti | |
| 1929 | 24–29 October 'Wall Street Crash' – collapse of the stock market | |
| | Presidency of Herbert Hoover began | |
| | Agricultural Marketing Act | |
| 1930 | Hawley-Smoot tariff | |
| 1932 | Reconstruction Finance Corporation set up | |
| | Emergency Relief and Construction Act | |
| | Bonus Army march on Washington | |
| | Hoover defeated in the presidential election | |
| 1933 | Presidency of Franklin Delano Roosevelt | |
| | Abolition of Prohibition | |
| | March | Emergency Banking Relief Act |
| | | Farm Credit Act |
| | | Civilian Conservation Corps |
| | May | Glass–Steagall Act |
| | | Truth in Securities Act |
| | | Agricultural Adjustment Act |
| | | Federal Emergency Relief Act |
| | June | National Industrial Recovery Act |
| | | National Recovery Administration |
| | | Public Works Administration |
| | November | Civil Works Administration |
| 1934 | Indian Reorganization Act | |

| | | |
|---|---|---|
| 1935 | April | Emergency Relief Appropriation Act |
| | May 25 | Black Monday |
| | June | Revenue (Wealth Tax) Act |
| | July | National Labor Relations Act |
| | August | Social Security Act |
| | | Banking Act |
| 1936 | Roosevelt's battle with the Supreme Court (Judiciary Reform Bill) | |
| 1937 | 'Roosevelt recession' | |
| 1940 | Smith Act | |
| | Selective Service Act | |
| 1942 | Executive Order 8802 | |
| 1943 | Smith–Connally War Labor Disputes Act | |
| | Race riots in Detroit | |
| 1944 | Roosevelt began his fourth term of office | |
| 1945 | Death of Roosevelt | |
| | Presidency of Harry Truman began | |
| | End of the Second World War | |
| | Economic Bill of Rights | |
| | GI Bill of Rights (Selective Service Man's Readjustment Act) | |
| 1946 | Employment Act | |
| 1947 | Taft-Hartley Act | |
| | Truman Doctrine or containment | |
| 1948 | Marshall Aid | |
| | Berlin Airlift began | |
| | China became Communist | |
| | USSR exploded its first atomic bomb | |
| 1950–53 | Korean War | |
| 1950 | McCarthy's anti-Communist 'witch-hunt' began | |
| 1954 | USA exploded its first hydrogen bomb | |
| | Brown v. Topeka ruling | |
| | Citizens' Councils formed | |
| 1955 | Murder of Emmet Till | |

# Mark scheme

## A01 mark scheme

- Analytical focus
- Accurate detail
- Supported judgement
- Argument and structure

| AS Marks | | A Level Marks |
|---|---|---|
| 1–4 | **Level 1**<br>• Simplistic, limited focus<br>• Limited detail, limited accuracy<br>• No judgement or asserted judgement<br>• Limited organisation, no argument | 1–3 |
| 5–10 | **Level 2**<br>• Descriptive, implicit focus<br>• Limited detail, mostly accurate<br>• Judgement with limited support<br>• Basic organisation, limited argument | 4–7 |
| 11–16 | **Level 3**<br>• Some analysis, clear focus (maybe descriptive in places)<br>• Some detail, mostly accurate<br>• Judgement with some support, based on implicit criteria<br>• Some organisation, the argument is broadly clear | |
| 17–20 | **Level 4**<br>• Clear analysis, clear focus (maybe uneven)<br>• Sufficient detail, mostly accurate<br>• Judgement with some support, based on valid criteria<br>• Generally well organised, logical argument (may lack precision) | 13–16 |
| | **Level 5**<br>• Sustained analysis, clear focus<br>• Sufficient accurate detail, fully answers the question<br>• Judgement with full support, based on valid criteria (considers relative significance)<br>• Well organised, logical argument communicated with precision | 17–20 |

# AO2 mark scheme – AS Level

- Source analysis
- Detail from context
- Evaluation of source material

| AS (a) Marks | | AS (b) Marks |
|---|---|---|
| 1–2 | **Level 1**<br>• Surface level comprehension of the source demonstrated through quoting and paraphrasing<br>• Some relevant knowledge, not linked to the source<br>• Limited evaluation of source material in relation to the enquiry, with simplistic support | 1–2 |
| 3–5 | **Level 2**<br>• Limited understanding of the source demonstrated through selection and summarising<br>• Some relevant knowledge, expands or confirms evidence from the source (or challenges source material in Part b)<br>• Evaluates the source material in relation to the enquiry, but with limited support | 3–5 |
| 6–8 | **Level 3**<br>• Understanding of the source demonstrated through selection, summarising and valid inferences<br>• Relevant knowledge, explains and expands on the source, and supports valid inferences (or challenges source material in Part b)<br>• Evaluates the source material in relation to the enquiry, by considering valid criteria such as the nature and origin of the source | 6–9 |
| | **Level 4**<br>• Analyses the source material demonstrated through an interrogation of the source to make reasoned inferences. Distinctions may be made between information and claim or opinion<br>• Relevant knowledge, discusses strengths and limitations of the source. Begins to consider the values and assumptions of the society from which the source is taken when interpreting the source<br>• Evaluates the source material in relation to the enquiry, by considering valid criteria to weigh the evidence. Some evaluation may lack support. | 10–12 |

# AO2 mark scheme – A Level

- Source analysis
- Detail from context
- Evaluation of source material

| | A Level marks |
|---|---|
| **Level 1**<br>- Surface level comprehension of the sources demonstrated through quoting and paraphrasing<br>- Some relevant knowledge, not linked to the sources<br>- Limited evaluation of source material in relation to the enquiry, with simplistic support | 1–3 |
| **Level 2**<br>- Some understanding of the sources demonstrated through summarising and making undeveloped inferences<br>- Some relevant knowledge, expands, confirms or challenges evidence from the sources<br>- Evaluates the source material in relation to the enquiry, but with limited or questionable support | 4–7 |
| **Level 3**<br>- Understanding of the sources demonstrated through selection, summarising and valid inferences<br>- Relevant knowledge, explains and expands on the sources, and supports or challenges valid inferences<br>- Evaluates the source material in relation to the enquiry, by considering valid criteria such as the nature and origin of the source | 8–12 |
| **Level 4**<br>- Analyses the sources demonstrated through an interrogation of the source to make reasoned inferences. Distinctions may be made between information and claim or opinion. Treatment of the sources may be uneven<br>- Relevant knowledge, discusses strengths and limitations of the source. Begins to consider the values and assumptions of the society from which the source is taken when interpreting the sources<br>- Evaluates the source material in relation to the enquiry, by considering valid criteria to weigh the evidence. Some evaluation may lack support | 13–16 |
| **Level 5**<br>- Analyses the sources demonstrated through a confident and discriminating interrogation of the source to make reasoned inferences. Distinctions may be made between information and claim or opinion<br>- Relevant knowledge, discusses strengths and limitations of the source. Considers the values and assumptions of the society from which the source is taken when interpreting the sources<br>- Evaluates the source material in relation to the enquiry, by considering valid criteria to weigh the evidence. Where appropriate, distinguishes between the degrees of certainty with which aspects of the sources can be used as the basis for claims. | 17–20 |

Quick quizzes at **www.hoddereducation.co.uk/myrevisionnotes**

# Answers

## Page 7, Spot the mistake

This answer would not get to Level 4 because it describes one example of technological advances without addressing the question of how far they were important in the development of 1920s prosperity.

## Page 13, Eliminate irrelevance

The problems of the Bull Market were to a large degree responsible for the Wall Street Crash of October 1929. The 1920s saw a huge growth in the buying and selling of shares, a situation known as the Bull Market. Many people bought shares, expecting their value to rise. Often they bought shares on the margin, or on credit. ~~Some lost track of how many shares they had or how much they were paying for them. They didn't understand the system and didn't understand they could still be left paying for valueless shares if their price on the Stock Market did fall~~. The Stock Market was unregulated, enabling unscrupulous brokers to speculate and practise insider dealing, thus enabling stocks prices to rise or fall artificially. They might do this by selling them to each other to raise prices and then agreeing to sell them all at once. Many would then be left with shares of little value. Clearly, the Stock Exchange was not built on solid foundations and if the economic boom collapsed, the value of shares would plummet. However, the Wall Street Crash was not caused by problems within the Stock Market itself. Other factors need to be considered.

## Page 15, RAG – rate the factors

**Warren Harding was elected the first of three successive Republican presidents in 1920.**

Many rural people distrusted social developments in urban areas.

Many people feared immigration and measures were taken to limit it.

Many more recent immigrants from Southern and Eastern Europe were suspected of Communist sympathies.

**There was a widespread 'Red Scare' in the early 1920s.**

**Attorney General Mitchell Palmer wanted to run for president.**

**Saccho and Vanzetti were accused of robbery and murder.**

## Page 17, Explain the difference

The first source is written by the leader of the Klan to justify its existence. He is using the historical development of the settlement of the USA to imply strongly that this was achieved by whites and goes from this to assert that different races should not mix. The second is from a Democratic politician who is attacking the Klan for hatred and prejudice and influencing government. It is suggesting that the USA should be tolerant of all groups and the Klan is in fact un-American in its activities. The historical context is the racism and fear of change, which was a feature of the 1920s. The Ku Klux Klan represented white, extremely conservative forces in society while the Democratic Party sought the support of all ethnic groups.

## Page 19, Explain the difference

The author of the first source is surprised by the number of women in the workforce, although he does not criticise it – indeed, he notes that while women have plentiful work they rarely rise to top positions. The second source, however, criticises 'modern women' for neglecting their traditional roles as homemakers. The provenance shows that the second source is written by a Catholic priest with conservative views who wishes to preserve traditional values, while the first is from an English writer and traveller who was fascinated by what he saw in the USA. The sources reflect the changes in 1920s society in terms of changing opportunities for women, which they view from their different perspectives – the priest condemns change, while the English writer observes and comments on it.

## Page 21, Identify an argument

Answer 1 contains an argument that is supported by evidence. Answer 2 simply lists points without reaching a clear conclusion.

## Page 23, Explain the difference

Garvey was a black leader who believed racial integration was doomed to failure and black Americans should join with other blacks to form a new homeland in Africa. He therefore supported racial separation and his organisation, the Universal Negro Improvement Society, campaigned for black Americans to leave the USA and return to Africa. These views were opposed by the NAACP, which advocated racial integration and sought civil rights for black Americans. Bagnall was a senior NAACP official in Detroit whose views were opposed to those of Garvey to the extent that he questioned Garvey's sanity.

## Page 25, Spot the inference

The first statement is an inference. The second and fourth summarise part of the source, while the third paraphrases it. The second statement cannot be justified from the source.

## Page 31, Identify an argument

The first answer is simply a description. The candidate might know a lot but they are not focusing it on the actual question. The second answer offers a balanced argument, with evidence to support it.

## Page 33, Highlighting integration

The second answer integrates the sources to give a focused response, while the first considers each source separately.

## Page 35, Explain the difference

Source 1 is the view of the incumbent president, so would be expected to take a more optimistic view of the economy and minimise the extent of the economic problems. However, it also dates from 1929, before the Depression spread. Perkins' account covers the period 1929 to 1933 when the Depression was at its worst, and she had experience of its hardships as Labor Commissioner in New York. While Hoover talks about the overall state of the economy, Perkins focuses on the human costs of the Depression. By contrast, Hoover seems bland and complacent – but you need to emphasise his conference was given before the worst of the Depression.

## Page 39, Identify an argument

The second answer contains an argument focused on the question about the attempts of the First New Deal to solve the Depression, while the first is simply a description of what was done.

## Page 39, Eliminate irrelevance

The First New Deal was successful in some ways and less successful in others. It was certainly successful in the level of activity that saw 16 alphabet agencies set up in the first hundred days, which aimed to solve problems caused by the Depression both in terms of recovery and relief. This activity marked a shift in terms of direct action. ~~Furthermore, Roosevelt understood that young people needed to gain experience of work. The Civilian Conservation Corps was formed to provide them with useful jobs, for example, in conservation in national parks, forests and public lands. By 1935 it had 500,000 recruits; among its work was the installation of 65,100 miles of telephone lines in inaccessible areas and planting 1.3 billion trees. It gave countless young men a new sense of self-respect and comradeship.~~

However, the agencies of the First New Deal were only partially successful in their aims. Many states refused to spend the monies allocated by FERA, for example, while the work creation schemes only provided temporary employment.

## Page 41, Spot the inference

The third statement contains an inference. The first merely paraphrases the source, while the second summarises it.

## Page 41, You're the examiner

This answer would receive a mark in Level 4. It contains accurate and relevant knowledge, and presents an overall judgement based on valid analysis that the First New Deal extended the role of government. However, the response is starting to get side-tracked by detail and as a result loses some of its structure.

## Page 45, The flaw in the argument

The argument appears to support the statement in the question, offering evidence in support, but then loses focus and goes on to suggest that it was Congress that led the way in helping previously neglected groups.

## Page 59, RAG – rate the source

### Source 1

… the National War Labor Board abolishes the classifications 'colored laborer' and 'white laborer' and reclassifies both simply as 'laborers' with the same rates of pay for all in that classification without discrimination on account of color. The Negro workers in this classification are hereby granted wage increases which place them on a basis of economic parity with the white workers in the same classification… This equalization of economic opportunity is not a violation of the sound American provision of differentials in pay for differences in skills. It is rather a bit of realization of the no less sound American principle of equal pay for equal work as one of those equal rights in the promise of American democracy regardless of color, race, sex, religion, or national origin.

… Economic and political discrimination on account of race or creed is in line with the Nazi program … The American answer to differences in color and creed is not a concentration camp but cooperation. The answer to human error is not terror but light and liberty under the moral law. By this light and liberty, the Negro has made a contribution in work and faith, song and story, laughter and struggle which are an enduring part of the spiritual heritage of America.

There is no more loyal group of our fellow citizens than the American Negroes, north and south.

### Source 2

Last week, without any public announcement or fanfare, the editors of *The Courier* introduced its war slogan – a double 'V' for a double victory to colored America. We did this advisedly because we wanted to test the response and popularity of such a slogan with our readers. The response has been overwhelming. Our office has been inundated with hundreds of telegrams and letters of congratulations proving that without any explanation, this slogan represents the true battle cry of colored America. **This week we gratefully acknowledge this voluntary response and offer the following: Americans all, are involved in a gigantic war effort to assure the victory for the cause of freedom- the four freedoms that have been so nobly expressed by President Roosevelt and Prime Minister Churchill. We, as colored Americans, are determined to protect our country, our form of government and the freedoms which we cherish for ourselves and the rest of the world, therefore we have adopted the Double 'V' war cry- victory over our enemies on the battlefields abroad. Thus in our fight for freedom we wage a two-pronged attack against our enslavers at home and those abroad who would enslave us.**

## Page 65, The flaw in the argument

The argument loses focus and strays into issues of relationships between those at home and their partners overseas, which could be made relevant in a separate paragraph but not as included here.

## Page 67, You're the examiner

This response confidently interrogates both sources by reasoned inferences, for example, how people couldn't opt out of rationing or fund raising. Relevant conceptual knowledge is deployed, such as the influence of radio and the persuasiveness of using stars to promote fund raising. This answer so far suggests a Level 5 response.

## Page 79, Spot the inference

- The third statement is an inference: the first is a simple summary: the second and fourth could not be justified by the source.

## Page 79, The flaw in the argument

Although this paragraph starts with a sharp focus, with relevant evidence in support, it goes into points about families that having nothing to do with prosperity.

## Page 83, You're the examiner

This paragraph is resonant of Level 5, both for its confidence and fluidity and the extent to which it suggests the infrastructure to combat fears was already present in the measures to tackle fascism. The key features of the question are addressed with valid evidence in support and the arguments are clear and precise.

## Page 87, Write the question

Your question could be on the lines of the impact of TV on the general public and in particular the influence of advertising. While the first source discusses the impact of TV on family life, it is also very much concerned with the impact of advertising. This is reinforced by the second source which is an extract from a code of practice: both sources acknowledge the power and influence of advertising on TV and the need for responsible and ethical practice.

# Notes

Quick quizzes at www.hoddereducation.co.uk/myrevisionnotes

Quick quizzes at www.hoddereducation.co.uk/myrevisionnotes